Alleluia!

A Gedenkschrift in Thanksgiving for the Life of Walter R. Bouman
(1929-2005)

Nancy M. Raabe and Ann M. Haut, editors

Lutheran University Press
Minneapolis, Minnesota

Alleluia!
*A Gedenkschrift in Thanksgiving
for the Life of Walter R. Bouman (1929-2005)*
Nancy M. Raabe and Ann M. Haut, *editors*

Copyright 2015 Lutheran University Press, an imprint of 1517 Media. All rights reserved. No part of this publication may be reproduced, stored in a retrieval system, or tranmitted in any form or by any means, electronic, mechanical, photocopying, recording, or otherwise, without written permission of the publisher:1517 Media permissions, PO Box 1209, Minneapolis, MN 55440-1209, or copyright@1517.media.

ISBN 978-1-942304-11-1

eISBN 978-1-942304-39-5

Table of Contents

Foreword 5
Stephen Paul Bouman

Preface and Acknowledgments..13
Ann M. Haut & Nancy Raabe

Poem 17
Anonymous

Part I: He is Risen!
Law and Gospel in Matthew: Implications for Hermeneutics 21
Mark Allan Powell

From Resurrection to Trinity..37
James M. Childs, Jr.

The Crisis of the Offertory:
A Treasured Conversation with Walter R. Bouman 51
Gordon W. Lathrop

Part II: He is Risen Indeed!
The Holy Spirit and the Church as Eschatological Community 67
Jonathan Linman

All of Life Is Sacramental: A New Way of Being and Seeing 87
Michael Rinehart

Walter Bouman: A Reflection 99
John Buchanan

Quintessentially Walter Bouman 107
J. Robert Wright

Part III: Alleluia!

Trinity: Why "Abba"? 111
Becky Robbins-Penniman

Misdirected Trust or Misfiring Neurons:
Theology and Science and a Study of Sin............................127
Anna Madsen

Motet, "I Shall Not Die, But Live" 140
Carl Schalk

Dying and Living 143
Nancy Raabe

Biography: Walter R. Bouman..155

Afterword..159
Andy Bouman

Appendix: Walter Bouman Selected Unpublished Writings

Partners in Proclamation..169

Sing to the Lord a *New* Song:
Music and the Mission of the Church 187

Final Sermon: The Rev. Dr. Walter R. Bouman...................200
For additional unpublished papers see walterbouman.com

Bibliography 209

Contributors...213

Editors...216

Endnotes...217

Foreword
Mass of the Resurrection
Walter Richard Bouman (1929-2005)

Sermon Delivered by
The Rev. Stephen Paul Bouman
August 23, 2005

The End of the Story

Then Jesus said to them, "Very truly, I tell you, it was not Moses who gave you the bread from heaven, but it is my Father who gives you the true bread from heaven. For the bread of God is that which comes down from heaven and gives life to the world." They said to him, "Sir, give us this bread always." Jesus said to them, "I am the bread of life. Whoever comes to me will never be hungry, and whoever believes in me will never be thirsty. But I said to you that you have seen me and yet do not believe. Everything that the Father gives me will come to me, and anyone who comes to me I will never drive away; for I have come down from heaven, not to do my own will, but the will of him who sent me. And this is the will of him who sent me, that I should lose nothing of all that he has given me, but raise it up on the last day. This is indeed the will of my Father, that all who see the Son and believe in him may have eternal life; and I will raise them up on the last day" (John 6:32-40).

A duck walks into a bar . . .

When Walter threatened not to show up at this affair if there were no jokes, I knew that I would have to go to two of my favorite theologians. Woody Allen, when asked if he thought there would be eternal life, said yes, with two reservations: Can you get there cross town by bus? And can they break a twenty? He also said that it is impossible for someone to be objective about one's own death and still carry a tune. I remember Walter's comments after receiving the diagnosis and the time he had left. "I'm counting," he said, echoing the great systematic theologian Yogi Berra who said, "it gets late early around here."

And the scale of this liturgy, a Cecile B. DeMille production spelled out in over five pages of instructions, the music, many guests, and especially the alb, stole, and chasuble in which he is vested reminds me of one of Walter's favorite comments, used often in his sermons. "My thrifty soul is cheered by the fact that I am getting my money's worth out of the vestments; and the ostentation of the liturgy is encouraged by Golda Meier's advice to one of her cabinet members: 'Don't be modest. You're not that great.'"

Those are the jokes, to assure that Walter is with us. And, of course, he is. He has chosen for the Gospel text John's version of the administration of the eucharist, the entire sixth chapter, giving us Jesus as the bread of life. Walter is with us, perhaps swapping jokes with the angels and archangels and all the company of heaven. In the series of incidents in John, chapter six, in which Jesus asserts that he is the Bread of Life, we find the present and the past (Moses and the manna in the wilderness) heavy with the weight of the future. And the people had difficulty understanding it.

The end of the story

On March 10, 2002, six months after the September 11 attacks there was a television special on the firefighters. The filmmakers were working on a documentary of life inside a firehouse. September 11 dawned as just another beautiful fall day. I was haunted as I watched them begin their day, the male camaraderie and joshing inside the house, the devotion to duty overlaid with boredom, the morning coffee and bagels, the quotidian gestures and conversation. But watching it, we knew what happened, what was waiting for them. We knew the outcome. It gave weight to every facial expression, every gesture, every breath they took. We breathed with them. The unbearable heaviness of being. It was heartbreaking to watch them race to the towers, then see them gather in the lobby because we knew they were planning and groping and rescuing in what would be the tomb of so many of them. The thud of falling bodies. Chaplain Michael Judge, his face a knot of concern. Then blackness. Then we saw his broken body gently and reverently laid on the altar of old St. Peter's, and as we watched we knew how many more would be borne up from the rubble. We witnessed the drama, knowing the end of the story.

Søren Kierkegaard said that purity of spirit is to will one thing. For all of the many intellectual, cultural, and theological eddies and streams that flowed out of the great river of Walter's pastoral and teaching ministry in the church, one strong, inexorable current fed them all. Walter saw that the resurrection of Jesus from the dead is the Ground Zero of human history and cosmic existence. He read human history the way he read detective novels. He knew that we know the ending! And it gives weight to every moment.

Walt, from a sermon preached at General Seminary in 1986:

> To be called to the mission of the reign of God is like reading the last chapter of a mystery novel without knowing the plot. That is, in fact, the way I read mysteries. I read enough at the beginning to find out who is murdered, who the main characters are. Then I skip to the last chapter to find out who did it. And that changes the way I read the novel.

Like watching doomed firefighters living out their lives in the shadow of Ground Zero, the Christian lives out of the knowledge of the paschal mystery. We know how it all turned out, how it will all turn out. This knowledge of Calvary and the empty tomb gives a weight, a portent to our everyday lives and ministry as well. We gather here in our sadness to be sure, already missing this larger-than-life gift to all of us, but we have read the last chapter. The Ground Zero of the resurrection of Jesus from the dead looms over every thought, song, gesture of farewell today. It adds weight to our time together and to every moment on our own homeward way. Knowing the end of the story means that we are laying to rest a conqueror today.

> In all these things we are more than conquerors through him who loved us, for I am certain that neither life nor death . . . shall separate us from the love of God in Christ Jesus, our Lord (Romans 8:37-38).

Blinded by the Light

> "Make no mistake: if he rose at all
> It was as his body:
> If the cell's dissolution did not reverse, the molecules reknit, the amino acids rekindle,
> The Church will fall.
> Let us not mock God with metaphor, analogy, sidestepping transcendence;
> Making of the event a parable, a sign painted in the faded credulity of earlier ages;
> Let us walk through the door."[1]

Like St. Paul, Walter was stunned by the resurrection of Jesus and never got over it. Walter, like Paul, experienced the resurrection of Jesus as both conversion and commissioning for ministry. I have been reflecting recently on Caravaggio's painting of the scene of the road to Damascus. Paul is flat on his back. Legs outstretched, arms raised up to heaven as he falls, his eyes shut since he has been blinded by the resurrection light. The central figure in the painting is the horse, which is shown sensitively lifting its hoof so as not to tread on the poor creature sprawled beneath its belly in the dust. The encounter with the Risen Lord is a devastating encounter that lays Paul to the ground in absolute vulnerability. Paul, and Walter, knew and taught that to follow Jesus, to live the baptismal adventure, is to be utterly dependent on grace, always ready to be broken again by encounter with the truth, unprotected, needy.

If Jesus beckons us beyond death, the future is open, and hope and promise are possible. This is how Walter interpreted the Reformation, as a pastoral call to get the end of the story right, to be vulnerable to the future beyond death, to give up death-denying justifications, to be placed by baptism into the death and resurrection of Jesus.

The resurrection of Jesus animates how Walter read and interpreted the Bible. Scripture is indispensable for the church because it gives us the narratives of Israel, the cross and resurrection of Jesus, the birth of the church. "Didn't our hearts burn within us. . . ."

The resurrection of Jesus animates why Walter loved the liturgy. Luther's *solus Christus* principle makes resurrection palpable at every liturgy. It is why texts and hymnody mattered to Walter. When he called on Lutherans to "take care of the chorale for the church because nobody else will do it for us," it was not denominational chauvinism, but care for these gifts in which we can rest in the paschal mystery.

The starting place for Walter's systematic theology is Paul in the dust, beholding the Risen Lord.

And the resurrection of Jesus anchored Walter's sense of the mission of the church in the world as eschatological church. Our engagement in issues of justice, peace, outreach to the most vulnerable, care of the earth, were not a leap from the central things of scripture, liturgy, sacrament, theology, pastoral practice—a long list of issues and causes tacked on to our life like bumper stickers—but propelled by them, animated by the resurrection of Jesus from the dead.

In our Gospel for today Jesus is giving the people a glimpse of a future beyond death. "I am the bread of life. Whoever comes to me will never be hungry, and whoever believes in me will never be thirsty… and this is the will of him who sent me, that I should lose nothing of all that he has given me, but raise it up on the last day. This is indeed the will of my Father, that all who see the son and believe in him may have eternal life; and I will raise them up on the last day" (John 6:35-40). As a *midrash* on the text he had just fed the five thousand.

What will be one day, beyond death, is here already in the life of the church. Someone quoted my grandfather, Victor Bartling, a teacher of New Testament at Concordia Seminary, St. Louis. They were studying Ephesians 2, where the author writes: "In Christ, God has already raised us from death to life, and has caused us to sit with Christ in heavenly places." The tense of both those verbs, "raised" and "caused to sit" are in the aorist tense in the Greek text. The aorist tense proclaims a decisive and unrepeatable event or action in the past. Suddenly Grandfather Victor paused and exclaimed: "Oh blessed aorist! It has already happened. In Christ we are already there in the gladness and glory of heaven."

I think this is why Walter was so drawn to literature, art, liturgy, drama. These are ways in which we glimpse heavenly places, when the stone of mortality is briefly rolled away and we are reminded of the end of the story. For Walter it was critical that the church be such a glimpse of the resurrection, of the future that Jesus promises. In seeking justice, standing with the oppressed, feeding the hungry, grappling with issues in this world, in its liturgy, sacraments, the church is the gate of heaven, eschatological embodiment of the promise of a future beyond death. The church knows the end of the story and lives it.

In an All Saints sermon Walter spoke of being in Leipzig in the Nikolaikirche, which held regular weekly events called *Musik und Besinnung* (Music and Meditation). He says, "I turned to a young man who sat next to me and I asked why he came. He replied, "The church is an island of truth and freedom. Coming here is like emigrating without leaving the country." Walter wrote: "I wanted to weep because it came as such a stunning revelation of astonishing power and truth."

Walter called the church to be such islands of truth and freedom, artisans of a vision of resurrection grace in Jesus, present in this life, beyond us in the open future on the other side of death: the Way, the Truth and the Life. And, by God's grace, many of us experienced Walter's presence, conversation, learnedness, passion, compassion, and humor, as an island of truth and freedom. Who else taught a class on Bach and Mahalia Jackson!

Foreword

The Bread of Life

In a remote region of Tanzania, I had the privilege of offering the eucharist to those who could not make the long journey to the church. The elderly, ill, disabled, vulnerable limped, were carried into the hut. They stretched out their hands for the bread of life, joyfully partaking in the meal of the resurrection. After the liturgy they lined up to have me sign the soiled, dirty yellow baptismal cards they were clutching, a lifetime of reception of the Bread of Life. They had little else in this world, yet they went away satisfied.

For Walter it all came together at the table. Let's not forget that we are remembering a sinner here today. When I called Walter after the diagnosis, he said that now he would be able to emotionally manipulate everyone around him. I said, "Walter, what's different?" His raucous laugh said it all. At the end of what he called his last great baptismal adventure, Walter stood before the Lord with nothing to offer except his vulnerability and his faith, his version of the yellow baptismal card and a lifetime of reception of the Bread of Life. And all his life, but acutely so in these past months, God surrounded him with a great cloud of witnesses who had to be willing themselves to be rendered powerless, with nothing to offer Walter and Janet and family except our own vulnerability and faith. We knew that he knew and trusted the end of the story. His dying was his greatest teaching, resting in the promises of the resurrection, waiting to be stunned one more time on the Damascus road home.

Several weeks ago I visited Janet and Walter. He had joined the disciples on that hill where Jesus fed the five thousand and promised the Bread of Life. Like the disciples he struggled to understand and to see the future to which Jesus was pointing. And like Peter, not understanding everything perfectly, Walter was living out Peter's leap of faith: "Lord to whom shall we go, you have the words of eternal life."

He asked me to teach his class with him. With pajamas, robe, and slippers he held forth, surrounded by his students in his living room. When I had to leave he asked me to bless him. He wanted his students to see that a bishop is a pastor at heart. I put my hands on his head and gave a blessing. He was weak and ready to complete the baptismal adventure. It was the last time I saw him in this world. So now, come to the table, where the end of the story is enacted once more. Walter is here, along with all of our loved ones whose baptism has carried them safely to the One who holds the future in his living hands. Christ has died. Christ is risen. Christ will come again. In a moment we will sing a hymn which always tears at my heart, "Lord let at last thine angels come" [Stanza 3 of "Lord, Thee I Love With All My Heart"]. At the table they are already here.

Let Walter's words from a sermon preached on Bach's communion cantata, *Schmücke dich, o liebe Seele,*[2] be our words of invitation:

> The eucharist marks us as belonging to Christ, as members of his community of hope and promise. The words of Johann Franck, the tune of Johann Crueger, the cantata of Johann Bach remind us that they belong to the vast company of heaven with whom we already feast in anticipation. The future is God's and therefore ours. Come to the feast.

Preface and Acknowledgments

The Rev. Dr. Walter R. Bouman, ThD (1929-2005), was a rare individual whose intellectual prowess and rigorous theological arguments were eclipsed only by his love of God. This compilation of essays is rightly called a *Gedenkschrift*, as we were advised early on by Robin Steinke, president of Luther Seminary and one of Walt's former students, for it celebrates posthumously the man to whom it is dedicated. We believe Walt himself would have acknowledged this detail, so we honor him here by beginning with a recognition of his appreciation for precise language.

Walt was often referred to as a man who was larger than life, who enjoyed a good scholarly argument, and who commanded attention. He was always respected, even by his detractors, and was well loved by colleagues and students.

In Chapter 3 of Volume 1 of his systematic theology, *Jesus is Risen: Theology for the Church*,[3] he is recorded as having said that "ultimate truth or final authentic historical meaning is known only from a story's final end, its ultimate outcome." Using himself as an example, he continued,

> I do not know the outcome of what I teach. I do not know its ripples, where they will go, what effect my teaching will have because I am not in control of your biographies, your destinies, your stories. I don't know what you will do with my work, and the people who are in my classes are going to do different things with what I teach! So the final outcome of my enterprise will not be known when I retire,

or when I die. It may not be known when you retire or die. It will be known when all the people whom you teach and all the people whom they teach ... well, until history reaches its *telos*. In other words, the final consequence of what I am engaged in, what we are engaged in, is going to be known only at the end. Because we are in the midst of history we can know ultimate meaning only if the outcome is given to us.

In this volume, readers are invited to enter into conversation with theologians whose work represents the dynamic search for truth that Walt once shared, and who continue in the enterprise to which he gave his life. The book begins with the funeral sermon delivered in 2005 by his nephew, Stephen Paul Bouman, for as Walt often said, to begin at the end of the story is to better understand its message. As such, readers are offered a glimpse into Walt's character through stories told about him at the end of his life.

The essays that follow represent the rigorous thinking that Walt would likely have enjoyed—whether or not he would have agreed, as the authors in this book often indicate. The volume is divided into three sections: Jesus is Risen!, He is Risen Indeed!, and Alleluia! In the first section, Jesus is Risen!, Mark Allan Powell, James M. Childs, Jr., and Gordon W. Lathrop, each a cherished colleague with whom Bouman worked and struggled in strengthening his own theological position, continue arguments on some of the topics in which he was engaged.

The second section's essays are by Jonathan Linman, Michael Rinehart, John Buchanan, and Robert Wright, who worked with Bouman on a variety of endeavors or were involved in teaching or leadership roles in the church or the academy.

In the third section, the outcome of some of Walt's teaching is seen in contributions from former students and colleagues Becky Robbins-Penniman and Anna Madsen. The chapter is rounded out by a new musical composition by Carl Schalk dedicated to Walt, and a reflection on the Schalk motet by Nancy Raabe. Both Schalk and Raabe recognize Bouman's love for and deep understanding of church music.

The volume concludes with Andy Bouman's family reflections on his father. This is a fitting end to a book that invites readers who knew Bouman to recall their own stories about the man who inspired students and colleagues alike to share God's promise given through Jesus of Nazareth. We include a few of Walt's unpublished papers in the Appendix.

Thanks must be extended here to Lutheran University Press for publishing this *Gedenkschrift*. We are deeply grateful to Karen Walhof, who graciously accepted the enormous task of making available this text and the two volumes of Walt's systematic theology, *Jesus is Risen! Theology for the Church,* also published this year. Proceeds from all three books go to the Walter R. and Janet A. Bouman Chair in Church Music at Trinity Lutheran Seminary.

Respectfully,
Ann M. Haut & Nancy Raabe
The Day of Pentecost, 2015

Poem

When I was a seminarian I used to love to read the *Saturday Evening Post* in the library. One issue contained a wonderful poem, actually a little bit of doggerel, for which I have always been grateful.

Walt Bouman

By daylight when I wishes to awe
My friends with my acumen,
How wittily I hem and haw
(To err is only human).
But when at night I lay abed,
And Morpheus treats me badly,
The clever things I should have said
Come trooping to me gladly.
Ah, what a killer I would be,
How deucedly attractive,
If repertoires of repartee
Were only retroactive!

Anonymous

Contributed by Luke Bouman

PART I
He is Risen!

Law and Gospel in Matthew
Implications for Hermeneutics[4]

Mark Allan Powell

Modern study of the Gospel of Matthew raises a number of hermeneutical questions that may be of particular concern to Lutherans. Many of these arise as a consequence of the attention this Gospel gives to the law, i.e., Torah.[5]

First, Matthew's Gospel makes clear that the entire law of Moses will remain in full force until heaven and earth pass away (5:18). There is no thought that believers enjoy a new dispensation in which they are no longer "under the law" (Romans 6:14; 1 Corinthians 9:20; Galatians 3:23); rather, the expectation seems to be that followers of Jesus will exhibit a higher righteousness, obeying even the most minute commandments of Torah in a way that puts the scribes and Pharisees to shame (5:20). Becoming a disciple means being taught to obey all the commandments of Jesus, which surely includes his command to do and keep everything that Moses taught (28:19–20; cf. 5:17–20; 23:2–3).

Further, Matthew's Gospel does not obviously espouse any theology of justification by grace through faith. God is merciful and willing to forgive trespasses, but the gate to the kingdom is narrow and the road that leads to life is hard (7:13–14). Trees that do not bear good fruit are cut down and thrown into the fire (7:19); God does not forgive the sins of those who hold grudges against others (6:15; 20; 18:34–35); everyone (baptized or not, believing or not) will be judged by God with the same standard they used when judging others (7:2); those who fail to take drastic measures (plucking out their eyes, severing their limbs) to insure they are living righteously will be thrown into hell (18:8–9). Much of this is metaphorical and can be read as prophetic rhetoric, but the bottom line seems to be that the primary entrance requirement for the kingdom of heaven is not "confessing faith in Jesus Christ as Lord" but "doing the will of God" (7:21).

There may have been a time when Lutherans could have dealt with "problem texts" in Matthew by citing verses that clarify matters in a manner more congenial to our theology. For example, Matthew 7:21 could be domesticated by application of John 6:29 (doing God's will *means* believing in Jesus Christ). But advances in exegetical science have rendered such casual solutions intolerable. Decades of historical criticism, especially redaction criticism, have left us with an almost indisputable conclusion: the author of Matthew's Gospel would not have agreed with the Apostle Paul on some fundamental matters of faith, nor would he have agreed with leaders of Lutheran churches on some key principles of Lutheran theology.

We must struggle with this realization in our ongoing discussions of hermeneutics. There could be Lutheran theologians who would dispute the contention, claiming that *rightly interpreted* Matthew's Gospel is fully supportive of good Pauline, Lutheran theology. I wish such theologians well, and I actually hope that they may someday convince me, but they have not convinced me yet, and I no longer think that they will. A more promising (but ultimately unsatisfying) approach simply seeks to minimize the damage, or to contextualize it in some manner that renders it less acute. Thus, some Lutheran theologians might appeal to a "canon within the canon" that relegates Matthew to the margins of what is deemed authoritative scripture, only valid when read in light of more certain truth. But is this a Gospel of straw? Is that the route we want to take?

At root, I think the problem lies in our relatively recent embrace of authorial intent as *the* hermeneutical key for finding authoritative meaning in scripture. The solution, I think, involves a de-throning of that particular hermeneutical principle in favor of openness to polyvalence and to recognition of the role that reception plays in the transference of meaning. Further, I believe the means for accomplishing this interpretive coup may involve a simple but effective application of our hermeneutic of law and gospel. But first we must recover that hermeneutic in its most powerful, original expression, before some questionable adjustments dulled its impact.

Law and Gospel:
An Audience-Oriented Hermeneutical Principle

The Lutheran idea of law and gospel is essentially an audience-oriented hermeneutical principle that celebrates polyvalence and locates meaning in reception rather than in authorial intent.[6] Of course, the principle was not originally articulated as such by Luther or his followers, but only the terminology I am using is anachronistic. Luther did believe and teach that the word of God was a dynamic force that impacted hearers; he essentially equated the *meaning* of God's word with the *effects* that it had upon those who received it. Of all the potential effects that God's word might have, two typical effects interested Luther the most: sometimes the word of God accuses and condemns those who hear it; other times it comforts and saves them. Those "typical effects of the word of God" are what Luther had in mind when he spoke of law and gospel.

In general, Lutheran theologians have recognized this. Carl Braaten says the law is that which "accuses, condemns, denounces, punishes, and kills"; the gospel is that which "comforts, strengthens, forgives, liberates, and renews."[7] Paul Althaus says, "The law places a man under the wrath of God; the gospel brings grace."[8] Our honoree, Walter Bouman, liked to speak of law as "existential dread" and gospel as "eschatological hope." His colleague at Trinity Lutheran Seminary, Don Luck, would describe law as "that which reveals our human brokenness" and gospel as "that which heals our human brokenness." Cheryl Peterson, the school's current systematic theologian, says, "The law convicts us; the gospel delivers us." I hope we can agree that these are different ways of talking about the same reality. And while people may prefer one set of terms to another, all of these descriptions seem to cohere with what I said when speaking of Luther's view in shorthand: the law accuses and judges / the gospel comforts and saves.[9]

It is worth remembering that "law and gospel" was developed with primary reference to preaching, not biblical interpretation. When Luther and others said that the "word of God" is both law and gospel, they usually meant that God's word ought to be *proclaimed* in a way that both accuses and comforts, judges and saves.[10] Of course, what can be said about the proclaimed word might also apply to the written word, and a hermeneutical principle for interpretation of scripture may be extracted from the "law and gospel" insight, but this has often been done in simplistic ways that are not helpful.

At the very least, we must affirm that "law and gospel" are not shorthand terms for genres of biblical literature. It is always reductionist and sometimes completely wrong to equate "law" with biblical commandments and "gospel" with biblical promises.[11] The word that accuses and condemns us might be anything that reveals God's majesty and holiness. Commandments often do this, insofar as they testify to God's standard of righteousness, in light of which all human endeavors are judged.[12] That makes us tremble, but so does any revelation of *who God is* when presented in stark contrast to *who we are*: God is powerful, we are weak; God is wise, we are foolish; God is omniscient, we are ignorant; God is eternal, we are finite; God is complex, we are simple; God is magnificent, we are petty, God is love (= fundamentally unselfish), we are self-absorbed. In sum, God is holy, we are sinful. And it is not just commandments that reveal the extent to which God is so different from us (and therefore fearsome and terrifying); the word of God always reveals this and, so, the word of God always carries the potential to accuse us and judge us.

Of course, the word also reveals that God comes to us, and it is not just promises that reveal this, but commandments as well. The word of God always reveals a God who is merciful and gracious, who takes the initiative in closing the considerable gap between us, who respects our weakness, tolerates our foolishness, transcends our finitude, and forgives our sins. Since the word of God always reveals *this* God, it always carries the potential to comfort and save us.

This is the original and powerful concept of law and gospel, a Lutheran hermeneutic that focuses on the impact God's word has on its audience. The concept underwent development, however, and some questionable adjustments to Luther's reception-oriented hermeneutic have not cohered well with author-oriented exegesis (particularly of the Old Testament and of the Gospel of Matthew). One prominent reinterpretation of the Lutheran hermeneutic of law and gospel appears in the Formula of Concord, which famously explains how the "law" has three uses: a *political function* of maintaining a semblance of order in society;[13] a *theological function* of showing people their need for the gospel;[14] and an *ethical* or *catechetical function* of teaching believers right from wrong. There has been a history of controversy in Lutheran theology over whether this "third use of the law" is actually valid. I believe I resolved that controversy elsewhere,[15] but, in any case, it need not concern us here. What does concern us is the subtle but highly significant semantic shift that has been made with regard to the word *law*. Obviously, the Formula means to say that there are three functions of biblical *commandments*; i.e., of "laws" (not of "the law" in the broader sense of any true revelation of God, which necessarily accuses and judges but which would not be necessarily didactic or, for that matter, politically relevant).[16] Thus "law" in "law and gospel" ends up being defined in terms of content (and, so, implicitly, in terms of authorial intention) rather than in terms of effect (and so, implicitly, in terms of reception).[17] This subtle but significant shift would create enormous hermeneutical problems for Lutherans, who sometimes resorted to desperate exegetical maneuvers in misguided attempts to make biblical texts fit into a mold that they thought the Lutheran paradigm required.

Biblical Exegesis: The "Lutheran Error"

Equation of "the law" with biblical commandments would prove responsible for what Joachim Jeremias termed "the Lutheran error" in exegesis of the Sermon on the Mount.[18] Consideration of this point will take us back to Matthew's Gospel and, eventually, lead to some concluding reflections on the hermeneutical problems associated with this book's apparent legalism.

In what would prove to be one of the most influential works on the Sermon on the Mount ever written, Joachim Jeremias discussed ways in which exegetes have sought to domesticate the ethical demands of Jesus so that those demands do not need to be taken seriously. For example, what Jeremias calls "the catholic error" suggests that the demands are not intended for all of Jesus' followers but only for a super-righteous few (saints, or clergy, or those who take special vows). More relevant to our concern, however, is "the Lutheran error," according to which the Sermon on the Mount is viewed as a ploy to expose the folly of works righteousness. Those who try to live the way Jesus demands in this Sermon will find that they are unable to do so; accordingly, they will be brought to despair and will be forced to abandon any hope of ever achieving righteousness through their own efforts. They will thus be prepared to hear the gospel.[19]

Centuries of Lutheran interpretation have embraced this reading, which was especially favored by Lutheran scholasticism.[20] To this day, I rarely lead a program on the Sermon on the Mount among Lutheran clergy at which at least one pastor does not ask "Wasn't the *reason* Jesus gave this sermon to make people realize they will never be able to live up to God's demands, so that they would have to trust in justification by faith?" But the answer to that question would be an obvious "No!" Historically, that was *not* the reason Jesus gave the Sermon on the Mount, nor was it the reason Matthew included this teaching of Jesus in his Gospel.

This was why Jeremias found the popular Lutheran interpretation of the Sermon so appalling: it contravened the obvious intention of Jesus, whom he took to be the author of the Sermon. What would we have to imagine? First, we would have to accept the proposition that the demands of the Sermon are not only harsh—but also *impossible to keep*.[21] Perhaps we could agree with that, but we would have to go further. We would also have to believe that Jesus knew his demands were impossible to keep and delivered them anyway, without any indication that this was the case. Basically, it was a trick, a big set-up to benefit later generations at the expense of his immediate audience. Jesus knew that someone would put his sermon in the Gospel of Matthew, which would be the first book in the New Testament, followed a few books later by Romans. Knowing all this, Jesus set things up in a very clever fashion, articulating God's will in a manner that would bring people to despair, knowing that if they only kept reading they would be rescued, in time, by Paul.[22]

I hope we can all agree that this is patently ridiculous. Still, we should note that it becomes ludicrous precisely because authorial intent is regarded as the final arbiter of acceptable meaning. Jeremias assumes that it is invalid for modern readers to hear the Sermon on the Mount in a manner distinct from that in which Jesus intended it to be heard. That assumption contains an enormous hermeneutical leap that, I contend, no Lutheran should be willing to make.

The generation after Jeremias tended to regard the "author" of the Sermon on the Mount as the evangelist responsible for our First Gospel. Even if much of the sermon derives from Q and probably reflects the actual teaching of the historical Jesus, the text that we now have is a Matthean composition and should be interpreted within the context of the Matthean corpus. Such an approach, however, only relocates Jeremias' objection without minimizing its substance. It seems obvious that the author of this Gospel did not intend for the Sermon to be read as a prelude to a more evangelical proclamation found elsewhere. Matthew almost certainly included the Sermon on the Mount in his Gospel because, like Jesus, he thought that people should live this way; indeed, he expected people to live this way and probably assumed that most people could live this way if they knew what was expected of them.

Questionable Hermeneutical Adjustments

Before we attempt a resolution to this problem, let us pause to describe the dilemma and analyze its causes.

The problem noted by Jeremias might be stated thus: Lutheran interpreters have often applied their hermeneutic of law and gospel to the Sermon on the Mount in order to produce an interpretation that is incongruent with the manner in which the author intended that text to be read.

This interpretation arises—and is deemed problematic—as a result of two questionable hermeneutical adjustments.

First, proponents of Lutheran scholasticism (following the lead of the Formula of Concord) reinterpreted the hermeneutic of law and gospel as applying to genres of biblical literature rather than to effects of proclamation. Thus, biblical commandments, including (especially) the moral imperatives of the Sermon on the Mount and of Matthew's Gospel in general were deemed quintessential examples of "law," and this meant that they had to function theologically to expose sin and instill despair, since that is one of the functions of "law"—indeed, its most important function. Apart from the misunderstanding that produced this necessity, the Sermon on the Mount would not have to be read as *law*—it could just as well be read as *gospel* (God's gracious revelation of how people can have a wonderful and meaningful life)—or it could simply be read as descriptive catechesis, or in any number of other ways.

Second, post-Enlightenment biblical scholarship established "authorial intent" as the arbiter for determining legitimate meaning, such that when the Sermon on the Mount is read as exposing sin and instilling despair, that reading must be deemed inauthentic because such was not the author's intention. But reader response criticism of the Bible now contends that, despite the obvious value of authorial intent in production of meaning, unanticipated responses to texts need not be deemed illegitimate. Indeed, reader response critics have demonstrated that the church has never actually been faithful to the hermeneutic of authorial intent that its scholars have espoused for the past few centuries. Isaiah 53 continues to be read on Good Friday, despite academic consensus that the historical Isaiah did not intend for his words to be understood as applying to a specific, future Galilean.[23] Further, New Testament authors do not apply any such hermeneutic in a restrictive manner. Where do we find Jesus or any New Testament author objecting to a biblical interpretation by saying, "That is not what Moses/Isaiah/whoever meant when they said this to their original audience"? And when Paul tells the Corinthians "the rock was Christ" (1 Corinthians 10:4), does he really mean to say that the historical author of Exodus (or Numbers) intended for his readers to understand that the rock was a metaphor for a future Messiah?

So, we have two "questionable hermeneutical adjustments" that have caused problems for Lutheran exegetes beholden to Luther's teaching that the word of God comes to us as both law and gospel. Both of these adjustments can be seen as cooperating to produce an interpretation of Matthew's Sermon on the Mount widely denounced as facetious.

Furthermore, the scholastic interpretation of the Sermon on the Mount is but one egregious example of the problems these adjustments create for Lutherans. On a broader level, we should challenge the ideology that allows a homiletical principle to control exegetical practice. I sometimes hear Lutheran church leaders maintain that since someone's interpretation of scripture does not cohere with "law and gospel," it must be rejected as a misunderstanding or an invalid use of scripture. "Lutherans are always supposed to interpret scripture in light of law and gospel," this person will say. No! I disagree. What we believe, as Lutherans, is that preachers should always *proclaim* scripture in light of law and gospel; accordingly, exegetical work that is intended to support proclamation should seek to interpret scripture in that light. But the concept of law and gospel should not be employed as a restrictive hermeneutic that invalidates exegesis of scripture for purposes other than preaching. The fact is, we study the Bible for many reasons and in many different ways. Sometimes, we simply want to know more about the ancient world: it is not wrong to learn about agricultural practices in ancient Israel just because that has little to contribute to the proclamation of law and gospel. More to the point, exegesis of scripture that sincerely seeks to discern the varied and contradictory intentions of diverse authors produces relevant data for catechesis and theology, and if such study is to have any integrity it must be conducted without imposition of any particular construct. Lutherans can affirm that the proclaimed word of God always comes to us as law and gospel without contending that every text of the Bible is properly interpreted only when it reveals those aspects of God's word.

Second, the hermeneutical assumption that texts are correctly interpreted only when they are read in light of authorial intent causes problems for Lutherans that go way beyond interpretation of the Sermon on the Mount. The simple fact of the matter is that the great majority of biblical texts were not intended by their authors to function as either law or gospel in the Lutheran sense of those terms. Some texts are merely informative: they were intended to relay information about practices, people, places, and things. Some texts were intended to explain various puzzles, such as the reason places or people are called by various names. Some texts were intended to serve as aids in worship; some were intended to offer moral instruction or just good practical advice. Some were probably intended to vilify opponents, or to advance the political careers of their authors, or to garner support for a given cause. Some texts were apparently intended to entertain readers or to evoke various emotional responses. If we were to apply our best exegetical methodologies for determining authorial intent and collect only those texts that were likely to have been intended by their authors to be heard as "words that accuse and condemn" or as "words that comfort and save," we would have a much shorter Bible, an ideal Lutheran lectionary, some might think, but nothing like the canon of writings we confess to be the authoritative and inspired word of God.

The historical critical method has served church and academy well in many ways, but it has not proved particularly helpful for preaching. Almost anyone who has taught in a Lutheran seminary is aware at some level of the potential tension between exegetical classes and homiletical ones. In exegetical classes, students learn to interpret the text in a way that reveals the author's original intent. And in homiletical classes those same students are urged to preach law and gospel in a manner that is faithfully evoked by that text. The problem is that, more often than not, the author's intent was not to evoke either law or gospel.

According to Lutheran homiletical theory, one should not simply preach the exegetically determined meaning of a text. An additional hermeneutical step is required, but seminaries have not done a stellar job of training people in how to take that step, and many pastors do not seem to have figured out how to do it on their own. What sometimes happens is that Lutheran preachers, just like other preachers, present the exegetically determined meaning of the text *as the sermon*. To my thinking, this might make for a fascinating Bible study, for inspirational and provocative *teaching*, but it does not necessarily make for proclamation of law and gospel.[24]

With the Gospel of Matthew, we tend to get didactic sermons, filled with exhortations, do's and don'ts regarding how we should or should not live as disciples of Christ.[25] I call these "so that" sermons. Martin Luther says in his Small Catechism, "We are to fear and love God *so that*. . ." and then lots of things follow. Especially during the Series A lectionary year, I often hear didactic sermons in Lutheran churches that are basically summaries of all the "so thats"; the preacher tells me what people who fear and love God ought to do. The problem with such a sermon, from my perspective as a sinner in need of law and gospel, is that it *assumes* I fear and love God. So, I tell my students at Trinity Lutheran Seminary, "Please! Do not make that assumption! Preach the law so that I will fear God and preach the gospel so that I will love God—and *then* I can come to the Adult Forum and learn about the 'so thats.'" Further, I tell them, "Do not think that just because I feared and loved God last week, we can skip over that part and get right to the 'so thats' for this week's sermon. I may be a worse sinner than you think. I know you are just trying to help me be faithful to God, and I appreciate that, but it is not what I need from a sermon. I need the word of God to operate as a means of grace, producing in me the fear of God and the love of God . . every week! . . law and gospel!"

Recovering "Law and Gospel" Through Reader Response Criticism

My contention is that the Lutheran concept of "law and gospel" actually assumes an audience-oriented or reader-response approach to scripture. It defines the meaning of scripture in terms of its effect on those who receive it.

Historical critical approaches to scripture assume an author-oriented hermeneutic: the meaning of any text is to be equated with the sense intended by its original author. Reader-response criticism, by contrast, seeks to discern the plurality of meaning that a text might generate for a variety of different readers who receive it in diverse contexts. There should be discernible trajectories between authorial intent and these diverse responses, but reader-response criticism does recognize that texts come to mean things that their authors did not specifically intend.[26]

As an official approach to biblical studies, reader-response criticism is only a few decades old, but Martin Luther appears to have been 500 years ahead of his time. His homiletical principle of law and gospel seems to assume an approach to exegetical interpretation that allows for a more dynamic concept of *meaning* than one that defines legitimate interpretation narrowly as expressions of explicit authorial intent. Reader-response criticism offers such an approach. The reader response critic attempts to recognize a *range* of possible meanings that a text might have in various contexts, and effects congruent with what Lutherans call "law" and "gospel" would typically be included within that range of possible meanings.[27]

Let me try to put this another way. Traditional, historical-critical exegesis focuses on discerning the intended *message* of a text, while reader-response criticism focuses on elucidating anticipated *effects* of a text. As we have seen, the application of historical criticism has caused hermeneutical problems for Lutherans because the *intended message* of a text (such as the Sermon on the Mount or almost any passage from Matthew's Gospel) might not have been to present a word that judges or a word that saves. But the goal of reader-response criticism is to elucidate *anticipated effects* of a text, which usually will include meanings that fit with the Lutheran principle of law and gospel.

Why? Because *law* and *gospel* are categories defined by *effect*, not by *message* or *genre* or *content*. Luther thought that any text could convey *either* law *or* gospel depending on the disposition of the audience.[28] This might become clearer with a couple of examples. Let's take the first of the Ten Commandments: "You shall have no other gods." Is that law or gospel? People who want to have other gods may indeed hear a word that accuses them and judges them. But people who *don't* want to have other gods, who find the notion of multiple gods oppressive, might take comfort in the offer of Yahweh to be the *only* God one needs to worship or serve. I can imagine any number of polytheists and idolaters throughout the ages who would respond to this commandment by saying, "Only *one* God? That's wonderful! I've spent my life trying to appease two dozen. This is good news." And, so: a *commandment* is good news = gospel!

Or take the beloved promises of the Twenty-third Psalm: the Lord will be our shepherd, lead us, guide us, protect us, provide for us. Surely that text is pure gospel, isn't it? Well, to those who want to be led and guided it is, but, there *are* people in this world who would prefer to just be footloose and fancy free, without anyone telling them where to go or what to do. To them, the recognition that they need a shepherd may come as a word of incrimination and judgment. Indeed, my guess is that most sheep, if we could interview them, probably would not *choose* to have shepherds. But then, they are sheep: they may not know that green pastures and still waters sometimes have to be provided, and they might not always give adequate consideration to what I would call "the wolf factor." In any case, the likening of our relationship to God as that of sheep to shepherd might be viewed as comforting and affirming to some and as insulting and confining to others. It might be received as good news or it might be received as a challenging word of judgment.

The hermeneutical concerns raised at the beginning of this paper are mitigated when reader-response criticism is employed as an exegetical strategy for discovering how biblical texts may be received as the word of God that speaks both law and gospel.

Rigorous application of historical critical exegesis leads to the recognition that the author of Matthew's Gospel had a different understanding of the law than would be embraced by Paul or Luther. He believed that the entire Jewish law (including, I think we must assume, prescription of circumcision) would remain in full force for God's people until the end of time. He further believed that the commandments of the law, even (or especially) as interpreted by Jesus could be obeyed and, indeed, would be obeyed by most of God's people most of the time. And he believed that, while the death of Jesus on the cross had made participation in the eschatological kingdom of God a possibility for all of God's people, obedience to God's commandments was still a pre-condition for anyone to gain actual admission.

According to my best reading of our first Gospel, the Matthean vision of what will happen at the end of time goes something like this: 1) most of those who do not confess Jesus as Lord will be gathered by the angels and tossed into the fire (cf. 13:41–42); apparently, no real judgment is required for those who did not know the Lord; 2) those who do confess Jesus as Lord will gain entrance to the final judgment where many (perhaps most) will be likewise condemned for their lack of moral righteousness (7:21–23); and 3) a few who know nothing of Jesus will be granted salvation anyway because of good works performed on behalf of those whom Jesus regarded as his siblings (25:34–40).

This is not the theology of the church, and no one should preach it. Still, it is instructive in many ways to realize with unflinching honesty that the canon contains such diversity. Matthew's Gospel becomes a testimony to an alternative variety of the Christian faith, a highly Jewish version similar in some respects to movements that Paul resisted, movements that actually prompted his deepest thinking regarding the law, justification, and grace. Historical-critical study of Matthew's Gospel helps us to understand Christian origins. We may benefit from this without assuming that "being faithful to scripture" or "believing the Bible" means adopting the mindset or even the theological perspective of the biblical author.

Reader-response criticism offers a different way: being faithful to scripture entails being affected by the texts in ways congruent with the author's intentions, albeit in ways that transcend those intentions to the extent that we are also affected by a fuller, canonical witness of scripture (and by sound theology based on that canonical witness). So, when I read the Sermon on the Mount in Matthew, I recognize that the author wants me to live in the manner so described—and I endeavor to do so. Over time, I experience some success, but much failure. It would be dismissive of Matthew simply to conclude that, since Paul says I'm justified by grace, it doesn't matter whether I live this way or not (cf. Romans 6:1). The Matthean Jesus clearly expects me to be able to live in the manner he describes and, ultimately, it is that expectation that drives me to despair. I am condemned not only by my own conscience or by the law of Moses but by the Gospel of Matthew and, quite possibly, by the historical Jesus. One has not experienced the full weight of the law's condemnation until one realizes that Jesus himself endorses it: I am damned not only according to Moses, but according to the Gospel of Matthew, and according to Jesus Christ (as Matthew, I suspect faithfully, presents him). *Now* I am ready to hear the gospel.

Contra Jeremias, I believe the so-called legalism of Matthew's Gospel *does* function to bring us to despair and prepare us for the gospel, but not because this was how the author intended it to function. This is consistent with the Lutheran concept of law and gospel, which was never intended as an exegetical principle for discerning the intended message of texts but as a hermeneutical principle for explicating the ultimate effect of texts. The Apostle Paul (who was no doubt Luther's primary inspiration for developing this concept) says in Romans 7 that the effect of the law is to magnify our sins in such a way that we are confronted with them: the law (in this case, as expressed through commandments) becomes the means through which sin deceives and kills, bringing death (Romans 7:7–11). But when Paul says this, he is not writing as an exegete, claiming that he has discerned the ingenious intention of Moses (or his biographers). He is simply describing the effect of God's word on sinful humanity.

Likewise, we Lutherans may recognize correctly that the paradigm of "law and gospel" summarizes the effects of scripture without assuming that those effects were explicitly intended in every instance by every author. The main point is that scripture *as a whole* conveys a message that accuses and condemns us, and also a message that comforts and saves us. With regard to the Sermon on the Mount and the Gospel of Matthew, it is not exegetically correct to say that Jesus preached this sermon in order to bring people to despair or to show them their need for the gospel; rather he preached that sermon in order to tell people how God wanted them to live, and Matthew incorporated the sermon into his Gospel because he believed people should and could live that way. Nevertheless, it *is* hermeneutically sound to say that despair would be an appropriate consequence of receiving the text as the words of a holy God spoken to sinful humanity.

From Resurrection to Trinity

James M. Childs, Jr.

All systematic theologians adopt a structure or overarching theological principle by which to organize and discuss the various *loci* of the church's theology. A classical example is the structuring theological principle, "grace perfects nature," in Thomas Aquinas's great synthesis of revelation and reason, *Summa Theologica*. The christocentric character of divine self-revelation was at the heart of Karl Barth's monumental *Church Dogmatics*. For Paul Tillich, one might argue, the organizing principle was his method of correlation.

For Walter Bouman the basis for his systematic theology was the gospel, the good news that comes forth from the resurrection of Jesus. So the title of his posthumously published theology is *Jesus Is Risen: Theology for the Church*.[29] Bouman proceeds from the gospel of the resurrected Christ in the first chapter to the doctrine of the Trinity in the concluding chapter of this volume. And, significantly, the Triune God is referred to as "the God of the Gospel: Father, Son, and Holy Spirit."

That we should move from resurrection to Trinity, as Walter did, is altogether appropriate from the standpoint of the history of the creedal development of the doctrine of the Trinity. It is the church's realization of and belief in Jesus's divinity that was the initiating force for trinitarian doctrine. Indeed, the resurrection was key to the church's understanding that this Jesus, the Christ, was truly God-with-us, a theme we shall return to later. For the present, we need simply recall the struggles that the church went through to consolidate the all-important dogma that the Son and the Father are one together with the

Holy Spirit. The success of that theological enterprise over against the threats of subordinationism, adoptionism, modalism, Sabellianism, and Arianism preserved the divinity of Jesus and his true humanity in unity with his divinity. In so doing, it preserved the critical claim of the Christian faith that none other than God Godself was at work in our flesh and our world to bring salvation to all creation. As a consequence we have an understanding of the Trinity and the unity of the works of the persons of the Trinity that is grounded in the gospel.

The subtitle of Bouman's systematic theology, *Theology for the Church*, also signals something that is basic to his work. Walter was, through and through, a theologian of the church. Despite his excellent academic credentials and the academic legitimacy of his work, his focus was not on the academy, but on theology for the mission and ministry of the church. I will be moving from resurrection to Trinity also in these few pages. In doing so, I hope also to be doing theology for the church. After a number of years as Joseph A. Sittler Professor of Theology and Ethics, I succeeded Walter as the Edward C. Fendt Professor of Systematic Theology, a development I'm happy to say of which Walter approved. The lecture I gave on the occasion of my installation in that position had as its subtitle, "Why Theology Matters." Theology mattered greatly to Walter. He was truly passionate about that vocation and the integrity of its endeavors. I believe that for him that "theology matters" was no less than a matter of life and death.

The Resurrection and the Kingdom of God

Matthew (4:23, 9:35) and Luke (8:1, 9:11) tell us that Jesus came preaching that the kingdom of God is at hand. His sayings and parables in all the synoptic gospels demonstrate the centrality of the kingdom of God in Jesus' teaching. In Luke 4:16-21 we read an account of Jesus reading the messianic prophecy from Isaiah 61 and associating its fulfillment with his own person. Matthew 11 records the visit of the disciples of John the Baptist asking if Jesus was truly the Messiah for whom John was preparing the way. "Are you the one who is to come, or are we to wait for another?" they asked. Jesus response: "Go tell John what you hear and see: the blind receive their sight, the lame walk and lepers are cleansed, the deaf hear, the dead are raised and the poor have good news brought to them" (vv. 4-5). Jesus is claiming for his works the work of the predicted Messiah in Isaiah 29:18-19; 35:5-6; and 61:1. Significantly, Jesus adds, "The dead are raised," an expectation not included in the Isaiah passages quoted, but by Jesus' time an eschatological expectation for the universal resurrection of the dead.

It is against the backdrop of prophetic and apocalyptic expectations and hopes for the arrival of God's reign and Jesus' identification of his own person and work with the fulfillment of those hopes that Wolfhart Pannenberg has placed the significance of the resurrection in his christology, *Jesus—God and Man*. For those in Jesus' time who shared those hopes for God's future kingdom, the meaning of the resurrection would be abundantly clear. It would vindicate Jesus' pre-Easter claims and provide the basis for faith in him. Pannenberg makes the following points[30]:

1. *If Jesus has been raised, the end of the world has begun.* The universal resurrection of the dead and the judgment are imminent. Christ is raised as the first fruits of those who have fallen asleep (1 Corinthians 15:20). [See also Romans 8:29; Colossians 1:18; Revelation 1:5.]

2. *If Jesus has been raised, this for a Jew can only mean that God himself has confirmed the pre-Easter activity of Jesus.* Jesus put himself in the place of God as, for example, in the antitheses of the Sermon on the Mount. This claim to divine authority, received by some as blasphemy, was vindicated by the resurrection.

3. *Through his resurrection from the dead, Jesus moved so close to the Son of Man that the insight became obvious: the Son of Man is none other than the man Jesus who will come again.* The Son of Man was to be a heavenly being, which Jesus now was as the resurrected one, who would come again in the future to bring in the universal resurrection of the dead.

> 4. *If Jesus, having been raised from the dead, is ascended to God and if thereby the end of the world has begun, then God is ultimately revealed in Jesus.* The resurrection of Jesus is the prolepsis of the eschatological kingdom of God; the ultimate future is made present in our present.

The resurrection of Jesus as the prolepsis of the eschatological kingdom of God is not only critical as the revelation of his divinity, but it also is critical for the revelation of and promise for the fulfillment of our true humanity in the image of God.[31] Genesis 1:26-27 is a break in the narrative of creation; other creatures are created through the mediation of the elements of earth, sky, and water, but humanity is created without mediation for a special relationship with God in the image and likeness of God. The thrust of "image" and "likeness" is one of dependent being. Humanity's very existence is determined by and grounded in its relationship to God. Moreover, the responsibility to represent God (this is implication of the Hebrew word for image: *tselem*) in the care of the creation signifies a personal relationship marked by freedom as the corollary of responsibility.

Although the few references to image in the Hebrew Scriptures refer to humanity, in the New Testament the phrase "image of God" is predominately a reference to Jesus' divinity. This is in keeping with what we have just seen in Pannenberg's theses that Jesus' resurrection reveals his divinity. Thus in Colossians 1:15-20 the christological affirmation concerning the image of God is that of Christ as preexistent image of God, as Creator and Cosmocrator (vv.15-17):

> He is the image of the invisible God, the firstborn of all creation; for in him all things in heaven and on earth were created, things visible and invisible, whether thrones or dominions or rulers or powers—all things have been created through him and for him. He himself is before all things, and in him all things hold together. He is the head of the body, the church; he is the beginning, the firstborn from the dead, so that he might come to have first place in everything. For in him all the fullness of God was pleased

to dwell, and through him God was pleased to reconcile to himself all things, whether on earth or in heaven, by making peace through the blood of his cross.

However, though we can speak of the image of God in reference to Jesus as a divine predicate in New Testament writings, we are also led to see the risen Christ as the prototype of our true humanity in the image of God. In 1 Corinthians 15:42-49 we discover that the focus for the ultimate hope for the fulfillment of our humanity, which is the fulfillment of our new creation in the image of God, is the resurrection:

> So it is with the resurrection of the dead. What is sown is perishable, what is raised is imperishable. It is sown in dishonor, it is raised in glory. It is sown in weakness, it is raised in power. It is sown a physical body, it is raised a spiritual body. If there is a physical body, there is also a spiritual body. Thus it is written, "The first man, Adam, became a living being"; the last Adam became a life-giving spirit. But it is not the spiritual that is first, but the physical, and then the spiritual. The first man was from the earth, a man of dust; the second man is from heaven. As was the man of dust, so are those who are of the dust; and as is the man of heaven, so are those who are of heaven. *Just as we have borne the image of the man of dust, we will also bear the image of the man of heaven.*

Our authentic humanity as image of God is revealed in the risen Christ, who in his true humanity is the first resurrected human being, the prolepsis of our fulfillment in the divine image. "Christ has been raised from the dead, the first fruits of those who have died" (1 Corinthians 15:20). Our creation in the image of God is in the fulfillment of our future in the kingdom of God. As we anticipate the realization of this promise: "... all of us, with unveiled faces, seeing the glory of the Lord as though reflected in a mirror, are being transformed into the same image from one degree of glory to another; for this comes from the Lord, the Spirit" (2 Corinthians 3:18). "For it is the God who said, 'Let light shine out of darkness,' who has shone in our hearts to give the light of the knowledge of the glory of God in the face of Jesus Christ" (v. 6).

From the perspective of the law in its accusing function, the theological use of the law, humanity's fallen estate in relation to humanity's creation, the divine image can be understood as rebellion against its own destiny in the kingdom of God. This is a far more profound understanding of sin than some older version of universal sin as loss of or damage to the image through the primordial sin of Adam and Eve. The loss of the image as a way of describing the consequence of the Fall is not biblically sustainable, especially when we realize that the fulfillment of all creation is in the coming future of God's reign.

Pannenberg in his early lectures on anthropology has spoken of sin as resistance to God's promised future instead of being open to trust in the promise of that future as the foundation of our lives. The contrast he draws is between security and trust. Security seeks to hold on to what one possesses in the present and, as such to be turned into oneself as one's true hope. Trust is open to the promise of God's future and ready to entrust one's life to it in the risks of faith and love.[32] Of course, this accords with the Reformation's view of sin as unfaith and, in Luther's famous observation, a state of being *incurvatus in se*, turned in upon oneself.

From the perspective of the gospel, humanity's hope for fulfillment in the image of God, fulfillment of the promise of creation to be one with God and each other in the bonds of love, is revealed in the resurrection of Jesus. The prolepsis of God's future reign in the resurrection victory is the foundation of hope calling us to faith active in love. The good news of the future revealed and sealed in the Easter event is that life has triumphed over death. The good news of God's future is that in that day the blind receive their sight, the lame walk, the lepers are cleansed, the poor hear good news, and captives and those oppressed are set free (Matthew 11:4-5; Luke 4:18-19). It will be a peaceable kingdom in which "the wolf will lie down with the lamb, the leopard shall lie down with the kid, the calf and the lion and the fatling together, and a little child shall lead them" (Isaiah 11:6). In that day we will realize what has been assured that "there is no longer Jew or Greek, there is no longer slave or free, there is no longer male and female; for all of you are one in Christ Jesus" (Galatians 3:28). In that day the whole creation will rejoice with us in freedom from bondage to decay (Romans 8:21). In that day we shall witness a new heaven and a new earth, one in which God will wipe every tear away and death will be no more, neither will pain or suffering intrude (Revelation 21:1-4). All this is from the atoning work of, to use Walter's formula, "the God of the Gospel—Father, Son, and Holy Spirit." And it is to the Trinity that we now turn.

Trinitarian Theology Today

Stanley Grenz begins his book, *Rediscovering the Triune God: The Trinity in Contemporary Theology*, by citing the comments made in 1972 by Jaroslav Pelikan and John P. Whelan, bemoaning the sad state of theology with particular reference to the theology of the Trinity. They saw the dogma of the Trinity as having become something of a museum piece with little or no relevance to the issues of contemporary life. This state of affairs they contrasted to the trinitarian debates of the first five centuries that were urgent and vital struggles for the very core of the faith. However, Grenz goes on to point us toward a renaissance of trinitarian theology that has been developing in recent times and to the theologians who have carried it forward and who are the subject of his book.[33]

We have already mentioned briefly at the beginning of this chapter Karl Barth's christocentric theology of revelation, his theology of the Word as the sole source and norm for our knowledge of God. However, this christocentrism was not at the expense of trinitarian theology. Barth moved trinitarian theology into prominence by virtue of the connection he made between the idea of revelation and the triunity of God. Grenz observes that, "Barth saw in God's triunity the structure present within the revelatory act of God in Christ."[34]

Another key contributor to renewed interest in the theology of the Trinity is the prominent Catholic theologian Karl Rahner. Rahner's concern was the way in which the doctrine of the Trinity has become isolated from the theology of salvation. "It speaks of the necessary metaphysical properties of God, and not very explicitly of God as experienced in salvation history in his free relations to his creatures."[35] For Rahner the Augustinian-Western tradition in Thomistic and neo-scholastic literature presents a "Trinity which is absolutely locked within itself...."[36]

The effect of this trinitarian isolation is to ontologically separate the immanent Trinity, transcendent and eternal in divine aseity, from the economic Trinity, God as revealed in history. Catherine Mowry LaCugna observed in her introduction to Rahner's *The Trinity*, "Many theologians who insist on an ontological difference between 'economic' and 'immanent' Trinity do so because they see no other way to preserve God's freedom 'not to create'."[37] The concern here is to safeguard divine independence from any notion that God has such an intimate relation to the creation that creating is a necessary expression of God's being. This not the issue Rahner was dealing with, LaCugna points out. However, it is a theological issue which Rahner's work addresses nonetheless. The ontological distinction between the immanent and economic Trinity poses the danger of a dualism that sets eternity over against history. This dualism is a sibling to the spirit/flesh dualism of the Greek tradition from which both ideas can be traced. Even though the Incarnation overcomes the spirit/flesh dualism, the eternity/history variety carries forward the danger of relativizing the earthly and historical in favor of the eternal and otherworldly. This sort of dualistic appraisal of reality has fostered a long tradition of otherworldly quietism.

Even though Rahner's primary concern was the connecting of trinitarian theology with soteriology, his famous "Rahner's Rule" speaks to the problematic of dualism as well. The "rule," which Rahner states under the heading of the "Axiomatic Unity of the 'Economic' and 'Immanent' Trinity" is: "The 'economic' Trinity is the 'immanent' Trinity and the 'immanent' Trinity is the 'economic' Trinity."[38] For Rahner this means "that no adequate distinction can be made between the doctrine of the Trinity and the doctrine of the economy of salvation."[39] The dualism I just cited is mitigated by Rahner's rule because the identity of the economic and immanent Trinity means that God's relationship to the world is intimate and internal to the divine life as implied by the Incarnation. As Ted Peters has pointed out, in light of Rahner's dictum, "the identity of God is shaped by the economy of the divine-human relationship taking place within time and history."[40]

Among those who have embraced Rahner's move and taken its implications even farther is the great German theologian, Jürgen Moltmann. Moltmann, with Pannenberg, was one of the most prominent theologians of the "theology of hope" school in which eschatological theology focused on the biblical prominence of hope for the kingdom of God. As we have seen Pannenberg's christology grounded in the eschatological promise of the kingdom of God, we shall see that Moltmann's theology of the Trinity comes to full flower in the arrival of God's future. (This is true also of Pannenberg's theology of the Trinity.) Given Moltmann's prominence in contemporary theology of the Trinity, we will focus on his account.

Moltmann makes clear the central importance of the doctrine of the Trinity in his comment on the heresies being dealt with by the ecumenical councils, starting with Nicaea in 325 AD—various forms of subordinationism in which only the Father is truly God or modalism in which Father, Son, and Holy Spirit are but different modes of the self-revelation of the one God who is a monad. Says Moltmann, "Both heresies are christological in nature. Consequently, the dogma of the Trinity was evolved out of christology. It is designed to preserve faith in Christ, the Son of God, and to direct the Christian hope towards full salvation in the divine fellowship. The doctrine of the Trinity cannot therefore be termed 'a speculation.' On the contrary, it is the theological premise for christology and soteriology."[41] Thus, gospel and Trinity are inextricably interwoven.

Athanasius led the charge on behalf of the trinitarian formula that would prevail at Nicaea over against the Arians. Rather than a simple monad, God is complex in trinitarian relationality that is proper to God's being. Thus, the three are one in essence and co-eternal in never-ending intimate interpenetration or "perichoresis" (*circumincessio*), a term we got from John of Damascus (655-750 A.D.) For Moltmann, perichoresis is key to a theology of the Trinity:

> John Damascene's profound doctrine of the eternal *perichoresis* or *circumincessio* of the Trinitarian persons ...grasps the circulatory character of the eternal divine life. An eternal life process takes place in the triune God through an exchange of energies. The Father exists in the Son, the Son in the Father, and both of them in the Spirit, just as the Spirit exists in both the Father and the Son. By virtue of their eternal love they live in one another to such an extent, and dwell in one another to such an extent that they are one. It is a process of most perfect and intense empathy. Precisely through the personal characteristics that distinguish them from one another, the Father, the Son, and the Spirit dwell in one another and communicate eternal life to one another. In the perichoresis the very thing which divides them becomes that which binds them together. The 'circulation' of the eternal divine life becomes perfect through the fellowship and unity of the three different persons in eternal love. In their perichoresis and because of it, the Trinitarian persons are not to be understood as three different individuals, who subsequently enter into relationship with one another (which is the customary reproach, under the name of 'tritheism'). But they are not, either, three modes of being or three repetitions of the One God, as the modalistic interpretation suggests. The doctrine of the perichoresis links together in a brilliant way the threeness and the unity, without reducing the threeness to the unity, or dissolving the unity in the threeness. The unity of the triunity lies in the eternal perichoresis of the Trinitarian persons. Interpreted perichoretically, the Trinitarian persons form their own unity by themselves in the circulation of the divine life.[42]

The emphasis on the three persons in perichoretic unity as the key to Trinitarian unity places Moltmann in the tradition of the Cappadocian fathers, Gregory of Nyssa, Gregory Nazianzus, and Basil the Great. Their stress was more on the relationality of the persons, while the West, since Augustine, has for the most part favored the stress on the unity of the "one substance." The idea that the works of each person of the Trinity are the works of all goes back to Augustine's formula, *opus trintatis indivisum ad extra.* Moltmann wants to dig a bit deeper. For him it is not simply that the creation is ascribed to the Father even though it is the work of the creation is whole Trinity. Rather the creation of the world is a product of the Father's eternal love for the Son and is ascribed to the whole Trinity.[43] *Opus trinitatis indivisum intra* also. When the Trinity is looked at in terms of the perichoretic relationality of the three persons in the bonds of love, God's love for the creation emanates from the very center of the divine life as an expression the God who is in God's very being, love. The perichoretic relationship of the persons of the Trinity in the divine life is echoed in a perichoretic relationship to the world. As God is love in the unity of divine relationality, so also in the relation to the creation, born of God's love and sustained by it.

This understanding of God's intimate relationship with the world, analogous to the perichoretic unity of the human and the divine in the Christ is foundational to Moltmann's concern to propose a doctrine of *theopathy*, the suffering of God.[44] As Luther once declared, ". . . since the divinity and humanity are one person in Christ, the Scriptures ascribe to the deity, because of this personal union, all that happens to the humanity and vice versa. . . . [Therefore] it is correct to talk about God's death. . . . If it is not true that God died for us, but only a man died, we are lost."[45] So, Moltmann: "If God were incapable of suffering in every respect, then he would also be incapable of love."[46]

For Moltmann the fullness of God's revelation as Trinity in unity with the creation is in the arrival of the eschatological event of the kingdom of God when God will be all in all (1 Corinthians 15:28). This will mean the transformation of all things, the realization of a new creation (Revelation 21:5).[47]

Some Implications for the Church Its Life and Teachings

In this section, we look at implications for atonement, the church, and the Christian life and ethic.

Atonement

As every first year theology student knows, there is no official doctrine of the atonement, no official theological rationale for how Christ's death and resurrection effects forgiveness of sins and salvation. Variety of theories have been proposed through the history of Christian thought, each having its strengths and weaknesses, and each having some biblical support. Some theories have seen Christ's death on the cross as some form of Christ making satisfaction for our sins. Still others have seen the atoning work of Christ as his victory over the forces of evil. Some have favored the idea of Christ as the moral teacher whose life transforms our lives. Because each has an element of truth with respect to biblical resources, theologians sometimes combine aspects of two or more of these theories. Clearly, there is a limit to how far we can go in our attempts to explain the mystery of why things happened as they did in the divine mystery of the Christ event. Meanwhile these various efforts will remain with us a faithful attempts to explore the biblical witness to the core of our faith.

What we have just seen in the discussion of the Trinity and the theopassionism of God's deep and intimate, virtually perichoretic relationship to the creation, enables us to add depth to our thinking about the atonement. As I have written elsewhere,

> In the Christ-event, God took into the divine life the sins of our resistance to our own true being as image of God, as well as the suffering, brokenness, and death that constitute our peaceless life apart from God, the source of life and the being of love itself. God does not ignore the truth of sin's evil and the tragedy of death. Instead, God takes it into God's own compassionate self that it may be conquered

as revealed in Christ's resurrection, which is the promise of our own resurrection and the fulfillment of our destiny of communion and union with God in the divine image. Because of God's "absorbing love," sin can be forgiven and life restored.[48]

Atonement is a function of God's love in solidarity with all creation and through the united acts of creation, redemption, and sanctification to bring it to the fullness of its perfection in the coming reign of God.

The Church

In the doctrine of the Trinity we understand the unity of the three persons in the one divine life to be a dynamic relational unity in which the Father, Son, and Spirit remain distinct—a unity in diversity—while yet participating in the very life of each other in the most intimate way imaginable: the mutual indwelling of perichoresis. It is not difficult to see the implication for the church, which confesses the Trinity in its corporate worship, that in the divine life is a pattern of unity and inclusivity that is its true catholicity. The Trinity in its relational unity is love, and the church by Jesus' command is called to love one another. Moltmann puts it this way:

> The perichoretic at-oneness of the triune God corresponds to the experience of the community of Christ, the community which the Spirit unites through respect, affection and love. The more open-mindedly people live with one another, for one another, and in one another in the fellowship of the Spirit, the more they will become one with the Son and the Father, and one in the Son and the Father (John 17: 21).[49]

The Christian Life and Ethic

If we are in the image of God by virtue of our destiny in God's promise, then we are *imago trinitatis*, formed in love, which is the dynamic of triunity, for the life of love. The self-giving love of God that excludes no one or anything in all creation and desires communion and union with God and harmony among all in creation is the economic Trinity that shows us the immanent Trinity. Regarding the further implications of this, I have written the following:

> Jesus, the crucified Christ is the one image of the invisible God, and, as such, Jürgen Moltmann maintains, reveals the glory of the Trinity in the community of his body and the fellowship with poor to whom he reached out. He goes on, then, to maintain that we need to think of our destiny for fulfillment in the image of God not simply in individual terms but also in social terms that reflect the divine life. Thus, the doctrine of the Trinity enables us to harmonize the personal and the social realities of our existence without sacrificing the one to the other. This an important theological insight for the church's witness to a society where the rights of the individual have often trumped the common good.[50]

So we may say that the church's witness in action and advocacy for a justice that includes all in freedom, peace, and abundant life—faith active in love seeking justice—is a witness to its trinitarian faith, which is to say, to the gospel.

Much more can be said about the themes of this brief treatise than is possible in this limited space. I hope however that when pastors approach preaching on Trinity Sunday they will be eager and excited about telling of how the doctrine of the Trinity is all about how God is with us in the most intimate, loving, and exciting ways one can imagine. Now here is something that is "awesome" in the true sense of that overused word!

The Crisis of the Offertory
A Treasured Conversation with Walter R. Bouman

Gordon W. Lathrop

In the summer of 2005 the telephone rang in my home, at that time in Philadelphia. My memory tells me that this call came early in August that year, thus only a few days before Walt Bouman died. And it was Walt himself on the phone, calling from what was becoming his deathbed. I had, of course, heard of the severity of his illness, and my wife and I were regularly praying for him. But now here he was in person, on the phone. I was very moved to hear his voice, moved to be able to talk with him directly at his initiative, moved at the stunning freedom and truth that the approach of death was giving to us both. I was also moved at the combination of strength and weakness of his voice. And I was not really surprised at finding myself more comforted in the faith by him, I am sure, than he was by me.

But he had not actually called to talk about life and death and faith—not even *his* life and death and faith. We certainly did so talk, though that was not his basic purpose. Rather, he had called to talk about the offertory.

Up until the last hours of his life, it seems, Walter R. Bouman, indefatigable teacher of the church, irrepressible and lively source of both orthodox theology and good humor, was caring about our common liturgical life. He knew that the new worship resource of the Evangelical Lutheran Church of America and the Evangelical Lutheran Church of Canada, *Evangelical Lutheran Worship* (ELW), was in the final stages of development before its scheduled publication in 2006. He also knew that I was a member of both the Renewing Worship Resource Proposal Group and the Holy Communion Editorial Team, committees that had been responsible for a penultimate development of much that was to be in the book. And he knew that I was his friend. Besides that, he knew also that I had written against too easy use of the ideas of "sacrifice" or "offering" in Christian liturgy[51] and that, along with my colleague Timothy Wengert, I had proposed that we might omit the use of the "offertory prayers" in the liturgy of the Holy Communion when it was celebrated at the seminary where we both taught. Walt was afraid that this idea was catching. He was worried that offertory prayers would be disappearing from the *ELW*, and he wanted to argue with me against that disappearance.

I loved the conversation. Or, at least when I could get beyond the pain of the circumstances, I loved it. We were immersed again in a lively and even loving theological exchange, not at all marked by polemics or suspicion or anger, about the meanings of Christian worship. Of course, he overestimated my influence on the forthcoming content of the book. Or perhaps he simply wanted to convince me of his position and so enlist me as an ally who, after his death, could continue to argue for offertory prayers in Lutheran practice as important symbolic expressions of "the stewardship of the world" and the doctrine of creation.[52]

He did not quite succeed. But then, he did not quite fail either. To make that clear I should say something more about offertory prayers.

What is called "the offertory" in Western Christian liturgy involves the moment in the rite when the bread and wine of the Holy Communion are placed upon the table of the assembly—the "altar." In the medieval Western church, that moment came to be interpreted by prayers and rituals, by an "offertory chant" and an "offertory collect" or "secret" (a prayer that was at one time prayed *sotto voce* by the priest), then by gestures of lifting and by a dialogue between the priest and the people (*"Orate, fratres . . ."*) about the "sacrifice" the priest was offering. That moment also came ultimately to be the time in which

The Crisis of the Offertory

the gifts brought by the assembly—the "offering"—were collected and presented, recalling an earlier time in Christianity when the whole assembly came to the church bringing food and money for distribution to the poor as well as for use in the eucharist. Associating that collection with the moment when the eucharistic table was set with bread and wine was a particular feature of Western liturgy.

Martin Luther, in his liturgical editing, rejected the whole thing. He did not reject the ancient custom of gathering food and money for the poor and for the bread and cup of communion; he refers to that practice with clear approval. But by the time of his work, such money as was collected was largely for the clergy and was intended to pay for masses to be said, thus seemingly to purchase prayers and sacrifices. And the setting out of the bread and wine of the eucharist was itself taken to be a gesture of sacrifice. In his essay on celebrating the Latin mass in Wittenberg, in which essay he evaluated and sorted the Western liturgical tradition for local evangelical use, Luther wrote: "... everything up to the Creed is ours ... [but] that utter abomination follows which forces all that precedes in the mass into its service and is, therefore, called the offertory. From here on almost everything smacks and savors of sacrifice. . . . Let us, therefore, repudiate everything that smacks of sacrifice."[53] Luther proposed simply preparing the food on the table, without comment or ritual, after the sermon and the creed and before the dialogue and thanksgiving of the Supper. He fiercely longed to make clear that the sacrament was not found in our offering anything to God, but in God's great gift to us. Even more, he taught that in the sacrament we are drawn into an amazing exchange—the *admirabile commercium*, the "happy exchange"—in which Christ gives to us his blessedness and his forgiveness, that we might in turn give mercy and help to our neighbor.

This exchange was not the usual expectation of religion, expressed in the phrase *do ut des*, "I give to you, God, so that you must be obligated to give to me!" Rather, it was just the opposite. "You, Lord Christ, beyond all expectation, give to me, so that I might turn to my neighbor in serving love."

Of course, Luther was also interested in the ways in which such giving to our neighbor might actually be assisted by the structures of the church. He argued for a "community chest," a common fund or "poor box," that should be supplied by those of the parish who had the resources and be maintained by the church elders, from which chest assistance to the poor might be given. He saw such giving as indeed arising out of the very faith that the Holy Communion fed, as arising from the happy exchange.[54] And, following his example, many of the written church orders of the Lutheran churches of the Reformation included regulations for the common chest in the very same writings that set down the liturgical order for Holy Communion and the rest of parish worship. Still, these liturgical orders did not ordinarily include collections ritually enacted during the service, nor did the overwhelming majority of them include offertory prayers.

Walt Bouman knew all of this. But he also knew that in North American church life a collection of money during worship had long been back in place. As it needed to be. In North America, the funding of the church and its mission, nearly from the beginning—after the dissolution of the bonds between church and state in New England and in Virginia and after the abolition of church owned "glebes" as a way to support the clergy in Virginia—has required strong local voluntary support. After attempting many ways to accomplish this support—"church dues" or "pew rent," for example—American Lutherans have rather universally decided upon what is called "stewardship" and upon giving money during the liturgy as an act of worship.

But, for Lutherans, that development has not been without difficulty. Taught by Luther, Lutherans have confessed that we have nothing to bring to God except our aching need. How do we express that truth and still practice responsible stewardship? When we call the collection of money in the church "the offering," how do we resist the idea that we are once again supporting the old exchange of human religion: *do ut des*? When, remembering ancient Christian practice and also newly accentuating God's good creation, we add the bringing of bread and wine to the altar to the actions of the offering, how do we avoid the idea that we are indeed *offering* the bread and wine to God? And how do we keep alive the ancient Christian idea, renewed again by Luther, that the church, formed by Christ's gift in the eucharist, will especially seek to make resources available to the needs of hungry people around us?

In the midst of the twentieth century, the Reformed theologian from the Taizé Community in France, Max Thurian, made a helpful contribution to the discussion. Writing about the ecumenical practice and meaning of the eucharist, he spoke of what he called "the crisis at the offertory."[55]

> Of itself the Church can neither offer nor present anything to God except its misery. . . . The Church's offertory, when it brings its material and spiritual goods to the altar, is a kind of movement, involving an offering, which precipitates a crisis. When the Church has gathered everything together to offer it to God, it realizes its poverty; there is nothing left for it to do but to remit this misery into the hands of Christ. . . .

For Thurian, Christ takes what we bring, together with our need—perhaps even takes what we bring as sign of our need!—and gathers this all into "his own sacrifice presented in intercession."[56] In the same writing, Thurian then explored how a few of the medieval offertory prayers—the *secreta*—brought at least something of this crisis to expression, by stressing human unworthiness to bring any gift at all. And earlier in the book, he expressed another side of this crisis:[57]

> The offering of material gifts to the Lord and the giving of them to the needy brethren [sic] are one and the same sacrifice: the memorial of the alms which ascends before God and then descends in blessing upon each one. The role of the offertory in the Eucharist cannot be too much stressed. It provides a powerful means of integrating the whole life of the believers and their brotherly charity with the eucharistic celebration itself.

For Thurian, the crisis, the giving to God, and the giving to our neighbor all belong together.

In fact, this very crisis of the offertory had long been brought to expression in the liturgies of American Lutheranism. The Common Service of the late nineteenth century, the liturgy that most influenced the diverse early twentieth century liturgical books of the many North American Lutheran churches, certainly had a collection of money, called an "offering," as part of its structure. There was no offertory prayer when the gifts were brought to the altar, but there was an offertory chant, to be sung by all of the assembly: an option of one of three psalm passages: Psalm 51:17-19b; Psalm 116:12-13, 18-19; or Psalm 51:10-12. Each of these three articulated the crisis, the first directly ("The sacrifices of God are a broken spirit."), the second with a question ("What shall I render to the Lord for all of his benefits to me?"), and the third—probably the one most widely used in American Lutheranism—with an appeal for cleansing and renewal, a clear acknowledgement that all we really bring is our need ("Create in me a clean heart, O God"). North American Lutherans reinstated a collection of funds, called it an "offering," and—at the same time, being Lutherans—realized a crisis was involved and needed to be expressed.

Then, in the mid-twentieth century, Luther Reed wrote of this liturgical practice of bringing offerings in procession and then singing an offertory verse:[58]

> The injection of prayers of blessing by the minister . . . impairs rather than enhances the impressiveness of the offering as an act of worship. Nothing is more impressive than the simple procedure of the officials of the congregation presenting the gifts of the people, and the minister offering them at the altar in quiet dignity, while the congregation stands in reverent silence. . . . The Offertory as we have it includes a selection of psalm verses or other permitted sentences. It is a substitute for the ancient custom, generally dropped before medieval times, of the offertory procession, as well as a substitute for the later medieval

feature which the Reformers deliberately rejected: the Offertory prayers.

But, in spite of this counsel of one of the most experienced of Lutheran liturgists, by the later decades of the twentieth century, offertory prayers were back in North American Lutheran practice. This was probably because of the continued need, among Lutherans, to strongly articulate the important idea of stewardship—we care for what God has given us, as responsible managers, not as owners—and thereby to celebrate how good it is to give. The use of such prayers began to happen even though the idea of the crisis of the offertory, as it had been expressed in the psalm verses that had become standard in Lutheran liturgy as offertory chants, might thereby be somewhat obscured. Thus, in the second order for eucharist in the *Worship Supplement* authorized by the Commission on Worship of the Lutheran Church—Missouri Synod in 1969, the entire assembly was to say this prayer after the bread and wine had been placed upon the altar and the money offerings placed upon the credence table:[59]

> Receive, O Father, these fruits of the earth, and the products of our labors, which we offer to you in token of the sacrifice of our lives. Accept them please, through Jesus Christ, our Lord.

It may be asked whether the crisis—our final inability to bring anything—is clear enough here. The phrase, "the sacrifice of our lives," recalls what Paul says in Romans 12:1, and it does so without any doubt or irony in the self-offering. Furthermore, nothing of the old theme connecting our collections to the needs of the poor comes to expression. What does seem to be the case, however, is that the whole assembly is called upon to speak these words with the sense that each person will thereby be paying attention, with the sense that the bringing of gifts is something we all do, not something done only by the priest, and with the hope that each person will be seeing this offering as one way that eucharistic practice connects to ordinary living and to the very stuff of creation. What does come to expression is a certain joy in giving and a joy in the goodness of the earth and of human work, both represented by the gifts.

Many of these same motives, as well as something close to this very wording, reemerged a decade later in the texts of the offertory prayers of the Holy Communion rite of the *Lutheran Book of Worship* (LBW). In the liturgy of that book, two alternate offertory chants were proposed, though only one of the "crisis" texts used in the Common Service, Psalm 116 ("What shall I render to the Lord . . ."), was still among them.[60] The other offertory verse, "Let the vineyards be fruitful . . .," a remarkable non-biblical but biblically eschatological text, written by John Arthur, turned out to be the most widely used of the two chants, however. That chant associated the offering with God's goodness in creation, with the "hopes and dreams of all people," with our related prayers, and with a prayer that the eucharistic table might "give us a foretaste of the feast to come." The offertory prayers then followed, and the book's two alternate texts, both of which were intended to be prayed aloud by all of the people, were these:[61]

> Merciful Father, we offer with joy and thanksgiving what you have first given us—our selves, our time, and our possessions, signs of your gracious love. Receive them for the sake of him who offered himself for us, Jesus Christ our Lord. Amen.

Or:

> Blessed are you, O Lord our God, maker of all things. Through your goodness you have blessed us with these gifts. With them we offer ourselves to your service and dedicate our lives to the care and redemption of all that you have made, for the sake of him who gave himself for us, Jesus Christ our Lord. Amen

It is these prayers that Walt was defending to me in that amazing phone call. And, in talking about them, we were inevitably talking about the crisis of the offertory.

For Walt, I think, our responsible stewardship of creation mattered a very great deal. Christians rightly take a world-affirming stance against all that would seek to exploit and degrade the world itself. For him, as can be seen in his posthumously published systematic theology,[62] these specific offertory texts expressly help us articulate that care, linking our reception of the eucharist to our daily lives. For him, "the offering of ourselves in the context of the eucharist" provided a liturgical locus for such earth-care, and came to expression especially in the second of the LBW offertory prayers, "Blessed are you . . ." But the first prayer, with its offering of "our selves, our time, and our possessions," those classic matters of Christian stewardship, grounded in Christ's self-offering, also at least implied the stewardship of creation.

While I do not actually now know, my guess would be that Walt felt that these LBW texts were stronger in this creation-emphasis than anything North American Lutherans had used before. He might have suggested that the earlier absence of an offertory prayer and the earlier Lutheran use of Psalm texts focused on the individual believer ("Create in *me*," "What shall *I* render . . .") might easily have led Lutherans to think that Christianity is largely an interior, individual thing about salvation, having nothing to do with creation. And the explicit expression of the crisis of the offertory—"The sacrifices of God are a broken spirit"—could too easily support an old Lutheran quietist misconception: there is nothing we can do anyway. I think Walt would have thought that the danger of Lutherans actually thinking we are bartering with God—*do ut des*—was significantly less than the danger that Lutherans would not see the importance of the communal stewardship of God's good creation. And, in any case, Luther's rejection of the offertory was probably out of date. For Walt, paying for masses was no longer such a problem, and he knew a lot of Anglican and Roman Catholic Christians, with whom he was in lively and important ecumenical dialogue, who could speak about "offering themselves together with Christ" and not be betraying the gospel.

I still hear his concerns, and I want to pay attention to his arguments. I, too, gladly sang "Let the vineyards" and gladly learned those two offertory prayers by heart. I loved that we brought bread and wine to the table, aware that God uses these very concrete things of the earth and of human culture to feed us with mercy in the body and blood of Jesus Christ. I certainly agree with Walt about the stewardship of creation, and find in this use of bread and wine a significant, earth-honoring impetus toward a more healthy economics: the care of the earth and the responsible sharing of resources.[63] And I was glad that, by being led by an assisting minister and spoken by all the assembly, the offertory prayers of the LBW were clearly distinguished from the Great Thanksgiving that followed

Only, for me, Luther's critique of the offertory, especially when linked with his interpretation of the "happy exchange," is still resonant, still brilliant. For me, it is still a religious idea that matters. And for me, the crisis of the offertory is exactly right: not an excuse to do nothing, bring nothing, care for nothing, but an awareness that, in the mercy of God, our giving gifts to others—that essential Christian act that must not be neglected—is not a demonstration of our great superiority, but most profoundly a sign of our need, rightly joined to the need of others. We rightly give to the poor and then come to communion as poor ourselves. As Paul says of the Macedonian churches: "their extreme poverty . . . overflowed in a wealth of generosity" (2 Corinthians 8:2), just as Jesus Christ "became poor, so that by his poverty you might become rich" (2 Corinthians 8:9). I think that all of our "self-offering" should be expressed with humility, with an awareness of our mixed motives and of our own need. The old religious motivations of bargaining with God are not gone. They raise their head all the time, still in need of correction, of the "broken spirit." Yes, we should give and give! But as unworthy servants, deeply aware of the pre-eminent giving of Christ that saves us and grounds all our giving, profoundly aware that the clearest "giving to God" is giving to the hungry poor.

So, for me, the LBW offertory ritual still needed some slight revision. It needed to express more clearly how our giving comes to its best meaning as it enters into the happy exchange. It needed to be clear that our financial giving here is not simply to maintain our own institutions, which we then call rather too grandly "giving to God," but that giving to God is always especially giving to the hungry other. It needed more humility. Yet, it also needed to avoid the sense—almost inevitable when prayers are made into communal choric speech—that the ritual was primarily about inculcating into our brains certain ideas about what we are doing. (For me, a communal prayer—unless it be the Lord's Prayer which we have learned from our baptism!—is best prayed by a single person, in words to which we can then freely assent—or not!—by our *Amen*.) It needed rather to express the crisis of the offertory, while maintaining its remarkable accents on creation.

So, Walt was right. Those LBW prayers were important expressions of themes that had been missing among us and that we should continue to welcome back. But Walt was also wrong. The ELW was not to be feared. Far from eliminating offertory prayers, such prayers were being published in the new book with a new strength.

The fascinating thing is that the ELW offertory rite represents a continuation of the LBW practice. "An offering is gathered for the mission of the church, including the care of those in need," the rubrics say. "During this time, the table is set. . . . After the offering is gathered, the assembly stands. Bread, wine, money, and other gifts may be brought forward."[64] Two possible offertory chants are the most obviously provided, "Let the vineyards" from the LBW and "Create in me," the most widely used of the old Common Service "crisis" chants from the Psalms.[65] And, with three options provided in place in the liturgical text and another six seasonal alternatives printed in "Prayers for Worship" (ELW 64), the ELW actually includes nine alternative "offering prayers." It is true that, in keeping with the ELW's generally permissive use for liturgical elements that are not essential, the use of the offering song and of the offering prayers is optional. And because there are so many, not easily memorized (and, perhaps to avoid the idea of prayer as the communal inculcation of ideas!), they are not appointed to be read aloud by the entire assembly. Still, as in the LBW, they are led by an assisting minister and they are thereby distinguished from the

Great Thanksgiving that follows. And, as in the LBW, the accent on the stewardship of creation is still quite alive.

But the really interesting thing is that, while continuing the LBW trajectory, the offering prayers of the ELW are yet more deeply anchored in Luther's critique of offering and in his ideas of the eucharist as participation in the happy exchange. The prayers ask God to gather us into that exchange. Four examples may suffice. The first prayer printed in place in the rite is this:

> Holy God, gracious and merciful, you bring forth food from the earth and nourish your whole creation. Turn our hearts toward those who hunger in any way, that all may know your care; and prepare us now to feast on the bread of life, Jesus Christ, our Savior and Lord. Amen.

The third prayer in place is:

> Blessed are you, O God, maker of all things. Through your goodness you have blessed us with these gifts: our selves, our time, and our possessions. Use us, and what we have gathered, in feeding the world with your love, through the one who gave himself for us, Jesus Christ, our Savior and Lord. Amen.

The prayer for Advent is:

> God of abundance, we bring before you the precious fruits of your creation, and with them our very lives. Teach us patience and hope as we care for all those in need until the coming of your Son, our Savior and Lord. Amen.

And the prayer for Christmas is:

> Good and loving God, we rejoice in the birth of Jesus, who came among the poor to bring the riches of your grace. As you have blessed us with your gifts. let them be blessing for others. With the trees of the field, with all earth and heaven, we shout for joy at the coming of your Son, Jesus Christ our Lord. Amen.

This articulation of the crisis and of the happy exchange is strengthened further in the ELW by the way it is paired with the "Prayers after Communion." In those prayers, the assembly begs for the Spirit so that it might live out what it has eaten, might be in deed what it has become in Christ's gift. Here are two examples:

> O God, we give you thanks that you have set before us this feast, the body and blood of your Son. By your Spirit strengthen us to serve all in need and to give ourselves away as bread for the hungry, through Jesus Christ our Lord. Amen.

And:

> O God, our life, our strength, our food, we give you thanks for sustaining us with the body and blood of your Son. By your Holy Spirit, enliven us to be his body in the world, that more and more we will give you praise and serve your earth and its many peoples, through Jesus Christ, our Savior and Lord. Amen.

In our conversation, I was able to tell Walt that these prayers were there in the book that was being published, that his concerns were being met.

Questions remain. The crisis will continue to raise them for us. Lutherans are not done with trying to figure out faithful liturgy and faithful gift-giving in our time. How do we express what we are doing in bringing gifts to the assembly of the church? How can that expression even more strongly celebrate God's good creation and call us to its care? How does that expression deepen our humility and turn us in Christ to our needy neighbors? More, unless we are serious in our giving to those who do really hunger in our world or in our response to this time of ecological crisis, how will our rhetoric be truthful? And today, how do we express any of this as we move away from a cash economy toward an increasing use of credit cards, even in the support of the church and its mission?

But for now, I have to say that I often think of Walter Bouman and that treasured conversation when these prayers—prayers I think that he would love and gladly use in his teaching—are prayed in the assemblies I attend.

And for now, in the mercy of God, may that beloved teacher rest in peace.

PART II
He is Risen Indeed!

The Holy Spirit and the Church as Eschatological Community

Jonathan Linman

Introduction

I had the privilege of my first acquaintance with Walter Bouman when I was but in high school and on a visit to Holden Village. Then I found myself at Trinity Seminary as a student where I encountered this engaging teacher again. Years later, as a professor and administrator at The General Theological Seminary in New York City, I was blessed with Walter's teaching presence yet again after his retirement, when we contracted with him to teach courses as a visiting professor. As student, mentee, friend, and ultimately colleague, my history with Walter has been one of ever deepening conversation, especially, as it turns out, about spirituality, the Holy Spirit, and the church in mission for the sake of the world. Now I have the privilege of extending our conversation via this essay beyond even the grave in celebration of Walter's theological life work, and in thanksgiving for Christ's victory over death.

What follows is a commentary on Acts 2:1-47, the Pentecost event and its aftermath, which seeks to correlate understandings of the Holy Spirit with Walter's theological perspectives, extending that thinking, and further exploring implications for seeing the church as eschatological community in mission today. In addition to reclaiming "spirit" as a meaningfully experiential word and theological category, a major focus of Walter's thinking about the Holy Spirit involves looking again and in greater depth at the biblical record pertaining to "spirit" and "Holy Spirit."⁶⁶ The commentary that follows attends to that rich biblical engagement, continuing an exploration of Acts 2 that Walter began in the volumes of his own work in the chapter that focuses on the Holy Spirit.⁶⁷

Moreover, there is a way in which you, the reader, might consider my efforts here an elaboration on Walter's definition of Holy Spirit. So I begin with his summary statement of his view of the Holy Spirit:

> The Holy Spirit is the promise of Jesus given to the eschatological community that we call "church." Wherever in this community we observe or experience the witness of the people to Jesus as Messiah—either in relationship to one another, or in relationship to the society, or in relationship to the whole created world: in the midst of all of these circumstances and events is the presence of the Holy Spirit.⁶⁸

The Holy Spirit Breaks In (Acts 2:1-13)

They were [sitting] all together in one place (v. 1).

Witness to Jesus as Messiah is a central outcome of the Pentecost event. Before we get there, though, a brief exploration of context is in order. At the end of Luke's Gospel, volume one of the Luke-Acts set, the risen Jesus had been made known in the breaking of bread (Luke 24:30-31, 35). But awareness of the resurrection did not yet result in public proclamation of Jesus as Lord. The disciples' hearts were burning within them to be sure, they told each other that Jesus had been raised (Luke 24:32-35), but as instructed, they were waiting in Jerusalem (Luke 24:48-49 and Acts 1:2-8). As Acts 2 begins, they were sitting, perhaps a significant posture in contrast to standing for public preaching, as we shall see (Acts 2:14). They were together, of one accord as the Greek suggests (*hapantes homothumadon*), in a particular place, perhaps the upper room where they engaged in constant prayer as the book of Acts opens (Acts 1:12-14). So prior to the in-breaking of the Holy Spirit is a prayerful stasis, though the disciples had engaged the organizational work of choosing Matthias to replace Judas as an apostle (Acts 1:15-26). The context for the coming of the Holy Spirit is thus communal oneness, not individualism—they were all together—a point central to Walter's understanding of the Holy Spirit. [69]

Also, the Holy Spirit's advent did not occur in the abstract, but in the spatial particularity of this world. Thus, prayerful waiting, unitive communality, and particularity of place and space are central features of biblical pneumatology in Acts, a perspective close to Walter's thinking that contrasts markedly with centuries-old and currently popular views of spirituality that focus on that which is individualistic, immaterial, and other-worldly.[70]

The day of Pentecost (v. 1)

Even as the Holy Spirit enters the community of disciples in a particular place, she comes at a particular time, the day of Pentecost, a day on the calendar of the chronological marking of time, but quite significantly also a liturgical festival. In the ancient Hebrew tradition, Pentecost was a celebration of the giving of the Law on Sinai. This day had come in the sense of fulfillment (*sumplerousthai*), not just that the day had arrived on the calendar scene. The day of Pentecost, thus, was not just any day, but an occasion of God's appointed time. Moreover, the coming of the Holy Spirit on what otherwise was a distinctly Jewish festival gives new meaning to this liturgical observance. In what would eventually become the Christian tradition, Pentecost loses its Law-oriented moorings, focusing now on the in-breaking of the Spirit and its effects on the community of hearers who would become believers.

Suddenly from heaven there came a sound like the rush of a violent wind and it filled the entire house (v. 2).

The Holy Spirit's coming embodies the element of surprise. It interrupts business as usual. Moreover, the Spirit comes from heaven, that is to say, *extra nos*, from outside of ourselves, from a place far away. This is a transcendent break-in. Note that biblical pneumatology in Acts is again counter-cultural to prevailing Platonic understandings in contemporary, self-preoccupied, popular Western culture. The Holy Spirit here does not well up from within the human self, from our innate capacities for self-transcendence. This is a point that Walter engages at some length in his exploration of new meanings of "spirit" and "Spirit," suggesting that the biblical witness contrasts with prevailing contemporary Western views that privilege interiority and which have existed even within the church for centuries.[71]

Furthermore, the Spirit comes as a sound. It is an auditory experience. This is enormously significant as the sound will soon birth speech, preaching, proclamation of God's mighty deeds. The aural nature of the Spirit's coming cannot be underestimated, a crucial feature of both biblical and Lutheran pneumatology, which locates so much of the Spirit's work in hearing God's living Word (Romans 10:13-17). Or as Luther quipped in the Church Postil of 1522: "The church is not a pen-house, but a mouth house."

The sound is a rush, conveying a sense of urgency, and one likened to a violent wind. Here recall the Spirit at creation as the creative wind of God that breathed order into the formless void of chaos. In its violence, this wind now makes for creative destruction in that the old order is being disrupted toward the creation of a new order where life, not death, has the final word.[72] Here are echoes of Walter's theology, which centers so much on the confident affirmation that in the risen Jesus death does not have the last word, a refrain I heard Walter employ again and again in preaching and teaching. The violent wind carries themes of judgment as Walter also suggests,[73] even as Jesus provocatively turned over the money-changers' tables in the temple (Matthew 21:12-13) as an occasion of enacted proclamation of God's reign, actions speaking louder than words.

Finally, the Spirit filled the *entire* house. That is to say, this is a holistic, comprehensive in-breaking. The Holy Spirit will not be compartmentalized, specialized, put into the idiosyncratic silos typical of analytical, reductionistic Western ways. In short, the Holy Spirit gets into everything. That is to say, the Spirit depicted here is not a dove perched in a niche up in one corner of the room.

Divided tongues, as of fire, appeared among them, and a tongue rested on each of them. All of them were filled with the Holy Spirit (v. 3-4a).

While the Spirit got into everything at the Pentecost event amidst the communal togetherness of the disciples, it is also true that the Spirit came to each of them individually, and in particular—divided tongues, differentiated consensus, unity in diversity—especially as this particularity relates to what will soon emerge as the ability to speak in the specific languages of diverse nations.

The Spirit breaks in via tongues—*glossai* in the Greek—also related to language, centering here on a speech event. These tongues are likened to fire, again evoking prophetic themes of a purifying fire that re-orders everything through judgment in the last, eschatological days. Moreover, these tongues appear *among* them, again reinforcing the theme that the Spirit does not well up from *within* the disciples. These tongues rested —sat (*ekathisen*)—on each, thus staking and making a claim, such that each will soon speak, as it were, *ex cathedra*, from a seat of en-Spirited wisdom and knowledge.

Even as each was visited, all were filled with the Holy Spirit. Not just the house was filled with the Spirit. Now via the tongues as of fire, each person was so filled. This is not a sprinkling, but a full immersion, a pouring, as into the vessels of their bodies as temples of the Holy Spirit in the thinking of Paul (1 Corinthians 6:19-20). Each and all, universal, inclusive, expansive—such is the in-breaking of the Spirit.

Moreover, this is not just any spirit, but the Holy Spirit of almighty God known through Jesus the Son, who called that God, *abba*, Father—a point about the Holy Spirit which is also close to Walter's heart and mind which ultimately views the Holy Spirit within the framework of the Trinity.[74]

[They] began to speak in other languages, as the Spirit gave them ability (v. 4b).

Here is a central focus of the Spirit's breaking in at Pentecost: this dynamic energy from God on high births speech. Throughout this passage in Acts 2:1-47, there are by my count some thirty-six words related to speech and proclamation— such as, address, declare, ask, hear, testify, listen, respond, call, prophesy, exhort, speak, say, voice. The tongues as of fire birth speaking other tongues in the form of language (the same Greek word, *glossai*, is employed for each, tongue and language). This is not speaking in tongues, which needs interpretation. Rather, this speech is in the readily intelligible languages of the nations. As the Spirit visited each disciple, that visitation came according to particular abilities, unique charisms, perhaps. The Greek (*apophtheggesthai*) also suggests that the Spirit gave them particular utterance, declamation, as if to say fulfilling a promise found elsewhere in scripture that the Spirit will give us a word to speak when we are called upon to testify (Luke 12:11-12).

At this sound the crowd [of devout Jews from every nation under heaven] gathered (v. 5-6a).

The auditory, aural event that is the Spirit's in-breaking does something; it has effects, namely in gathering a crowd of listeners, lots of people of Jewish descent, but from every known nation at the time. The people recognized something going on that transcended themselves and business as usual. It was for them perhaps a spirit—in the sense that Walter understands "team spirit"—that transcended the disciples' usual capacities, the whole being greater than the sum of the parts.[75] The crowd that gathered was likewise a whole greater than its parts as this group is multi-national, multi-cultural, multi-linguistic. It is thus catholic, universal, a representation of a wide mission field to which the gospel is about to be preached.

In our own languages we hear them speaking about God's deeds of power (v. 11b).

Members of the gathered crowd heard in their own native tongue proclamation of God's deeds of power—their own languages, the scandal of particularity. How else can the gospel be proclaimed except in the languages that the nations speak? It cannot be otherwise. It has always been so. Once again, the Spirit, and its effects in creating proclamation, comes to particular places, particular times, particular people, and of necessity, therefore, via languages intelligible to us. There is thus no room for any secret Gnostic insight here. The Spirit's work is that of translation. Sound becomes speech, intelligibility, proclamation. So it has been that the gospel has been translated throughout the centuries into virtually every human tongue, the Spirit guiding us even now into all truth (John 16:12-13). This work is the very opposite of the Tower of Babel when language was the source of division and confusion. Now language brings diverse peoples together under a unifying message, a point that Walter makes about the Pentecost event.[76]

The message here is about God's deeds of power in raising Jesus from the dead that he might be understood and proclaimed as messiah. As we shall see, this speech making is not just *about* divine activity, it *is* the thing itself, en-Spirited divine in-breaking that re-orients the world of the hearers who became believers. Speaking God's deeds of power in other languages is thus itself a deed of power, words doing what they say.

Bewildered, amazed, astonished, perplexed, sneering, they said to one another, "What does this mean?" and "They are filled with new wine" (cf. v. 6, 7, 12-13).

The Holy Spirit is here doing a new thing in breaking down the dividing walls of language, and by extension, national culture, and perhaps also ethnicity. The newness of this creative disruption understandably provokes a wide range of reactions—to wit, bewilderment, amazement, astonishment, perplexity, and, in some cases, sneering. But quite importantly, native-tongue-speech about God's deeds of power—that mere Galileans were undertaking this to boot—births another impulse, the desire to interpret, to engage in hermeneutics: "What does this mean?" There are those, of course, who resist the hermeneutical impulse and quickly, defensively, and dismissively conclude, "They are filled with new wine." For these hearers, human business as usual—a propensity for intoxication—is sufficient to explain away what is going on.

In the Power of the Spirit, Peter Witnesses to Jesus as Messiah (Acts 2:14-36)

Peter, standing with the eleven, raised his voice and addressed them (v. 14a).

The Holy Spirit, the power from on high, gets Peter up out of his seat. God's Spirit has the effect of setting us in motion. Peter moved from prayerful sitting to standing in raising his voice for proclamation. While his would be a solo voice, he stands in the company of his colleagues, a lovely way to re-image preaching for today. We never do it alone, but in the company of all the saints. Prior to this point, Peter's public voice was mute. "Up weak knees,"[77] the Spirit will give a Word, unleashing Peter's tongue! What begins now is the first public witness to Jesus as Messiah, who may be confessed as Lord because he has been raised from the dead, a point central to Walter's theology about Jesus as Messiah.[78] Among Peter's first words of this first sermon of the in-breaking new era hit head-on the skepticism of some of the hearers of the Pentecost commotion. Like Walter's lectures, Peter began with a kind of joke: "Indeed, these are not drunk, as you suppose, for it is only nine o'clock in the morning" (Acts 2:15). With ironic humor, Peter challenges the prevailing assumptions about the source of Galileans speaking intelligibly now in languages before unknown to them.

This is what was spoken by the prophet Joel (v. 16).

Peter's en-Spirited homiletical method employs the use of sacred scripture to interpret the amazing, astonishing, bewildering, perplexing goings-on of the day. The Spirit gives him the ability to remember and quote at length portions of the prophet Joel to shed interpretive light on the meaning of God's deeds of power being proclaimed in a multiplicity of languages (Acts 2:16-21). He goes on to make reference also to the Psalms of David (Acts 2:25-31; 35), further engaging scripture for the sake of understanding what has happened. Peter here is not indulging in mere proof-texting. Rather, he uses scripture as a foundation on which to engage in constructive theology, the very building blocks of what would become the Christian *kerygma* and the whole of Christian theology.

In the last days . . . the Lord's great and glorious day (cf. v 17a, 20b).

Central to Peter's theologizing is an eschatological focus and tone—again, quoting the prophet Joel, "the last days" (v. 17a) and "the Lord's great and glorious day" (v. 20b). In brief, the thrust of Peter's sermon suggests that the in-breaking of the promised Holy Spirit ushers in a new day, a new era, indeed the last great and glorious days of God. There is also an apocalyptic flavor to what Peter remembers from Joel's prophecy, adding to the eschatological thrust: "And I will show portents in the heaven above and signs on the earth below, blood, and fire, and smoky mist. The sun shall be turned to darkness and the moon to blood, before the coming of the Lord's great and glorious day" (19-20).

I will pour out my Spirit upon all flesh, and your sons and your daughters shall prophesy, and your young men shall see visions, and your old men shall dream dreams. Even upon my slaves, both men and women, in those days I will pour out my Spirit; and they shall prophesy (v. 17b-18).

The new era initiated by the coming of the Spirit on Pentecost is proclaimed to all nations, and within those nations it is intended for all people. The message is inclusive, expansive, if you will, catholic, universal—all flesh, sons, daughters, young and old men, slaves and women—in short, everyone, even those who had traditionally been excluded from community. Even they shall receive the gift of the Holy Spirit for prophecy, for proclaiming good news in prophetic terms. This vision of inclusion, like the coming of the Spirit itself, turns the world and its assumptions and operating principles upside down. Thus, the dawning new age breaks down old walls that divide and addresses age-old injustices that made for exclusion of many sorts, especially those most marginalized—women, children, slaves—features of the messianic age that Walter emphasizes.[79]

Prophecy by all people will focus not on prediction of the future, for that future has already come! Rather, such prophecy will center on the *announcement* of God's mighty deeds, another point dear to Walter's heart and mind.[80]

Then everyone who calls on the name of the Lord shall be saved (v. 21).

This in-breaking new age makes for salvation for everyone; again, it is catholic, universal. Like the prophetic proclamation of the mighty deeds of God itself, the gift of salvation is speech-oriented—it involves *calling* on the name of the Lord.

This Jesus God raised up. . . . God has made him both Lord and Messiah (v 32a, 36b).

Here is the core of the message, at the heart of Peter's sermon and undoubtedly central to what was uttered in the languages of the nations: God has raised Jesus of Nazareth from the dead and thus has made him Lord and Messiah. When this message is proclaimed, this, according to Walter, is also the very definition of Holy Spirit, an evidence of the Spirit's visitation. That is to say, when the risen Jesus is proclaimed as Messiah, this is the Holy Spirit.[81] Such proclamation is the Word that the Holy Spirit gives to Peter and the others to speak to the nations. Biblical pneumatology in Acts thus again centers on Jesus, the one whom God sent into the world for the world's sake. The Spirit's visitation is all about discerning the meanings of the events of Jesus' life, especially the final days, the death and the empty tomb. Or as Walter writes:

> The function of leading the disciples into all truth ("inspiration") refers to insight into what they have experienced (John 16:13-15). This does not mean that they will receive thoughts they didn't think before; rather, *they will understand in a new way.* They will see what the crucifixion and resurrection were all about. They will experience that "Aha!" moment—an "Aha!" about the redemptive nature of Jesus as crucified messiah: *that's* Holy Spirit, *that's* inspiration.[82]

Such inspiration is what is beginning to occur in Peter's Pentecost sermon.

We also have here perhaps the stirrings and hints of what would emerge via the Spirit's guiding as a trinitarian theology: the three persons of the Godhead in this passage from Acts are invoked, God, Jesus, Spirit. There is a long way to go before the doctrine of the Holy Trinity is in full blossom, but perhaps the seed is planted here, as elsewhere in the scriptural witness. Moreover, Peter's affirmations in verses 22-24 have creedal overtones, laying a foundation for the creeds of the church, which would be forged also by the Spirit's guiding.

Of that all of us are witnesses (v. 32b).

To witness to Jesus as Messiah and Lord, him having been raised from the dead, is what lies at the heart of speech-making leadership in what soon will emerge as the eschatological community, the church. The Spirit's break-in at Pentecost unleashes tongues, marking a transition, perhaps, from being disciples (students) to being apostles (ones sent by God to do the work of teaching through proclamation). Such proclamatory ministry in the public arena will, as has history shown, also make most of them martyrs (but in the Greek, simply "witnesses").

En-Spirited Proclamation Births a New Order in Eschatological Community (Acts 2:32-47)

This much is clear thus far: the Holy Spirit's breaking into the world at Pentecost releases tongues to birth proclamation of the risen Jesus as Messiah. This concluding section of this essay will explore the effects of proclamation, namely that proclamation then also gives birth to the eschatological community that is the church. The final section of Acts 2 reveals the characteristics and qualities of this eschatological community, its life, and its mission. The listing of these characteristics and qualities will be very familiar to anyone who shares in the life of the church even today. The conclusion of Acts 2 demonstrates, in short, a vision of the very reign of God known in the activities of the church and the qualities of its life. Furthermore, the very *ordo* of the church's life begins to bring the reign of God into the world. Churchly life, centered on the liturgy, is in the view of Walter's theology the "down payment" as a gift from God that allows us to live the reign of God even now, albeit in unconsummated, imperfect ways.[83] Or as Walter puts it in a very earthy, accessible manner: "When you make the down payment on a house, you move in. When you make the down payment on a car, you drive it off the lot, and zip down the eschatological highway. You act as if you already own them; they are already 'yours.'"[84]

[Peter] testified with many other arguments and exhorted them (v. 40a).

One foundational feature of life in the eschatological community is ongoing proclamation. Proclamation does not end with Peter's sermon. That monologue spilled over into many other expressions of witness, testimony, arguments, and exhortation, an expansive view of proclamation that encompasses far more than the traditional monologue sermon. Proclamation thus comes in many forms that are contextually appropriate for the time. Significant here is the notion of argument, that Peter made arguments for his en-Spirited conclusion that the risen Jesus is Messiah and Lord. Perhaps we do well to embrace apologetics as a fruit of the Spirit's coming and to see the Spirit at work in our efforts at making sense of the Christian witness for our own time. Such an impulse arguably drove Walter's whole teaching ministry, certainly as evidenced in his explorations of "spirit" and "Spirit."

Now when they heard this, they were cut to the heart and said . . . "what should we do?" (v. 37).

Peter's proclamation in its many forms has effects on the hearers—again, note the centrality of aurality, faith coming via hearing (Romans 10:17)—namely, that they are cut to the heart, or we might say, are filled with compunction upon hearing Peter's exhortations. En-Spirited proclamation cuts through the multiplicity of defense mechanisms—for example, the sneering conclusion that the Galileans were drunk—and provokes openness to the new thing happening here.

Furthermore, the effects of proclamation include wanting to engage in activity: "What should we *do*?" The Holy Spirit's coming and the resultant proclamation of the gospel as the very dynamism or power of God creates movement from nouns to verbs, from stasis to activity. The

Spirit's stirring is like that. Being cut to the heart with motivation to act is thus another feature of life in eschatological community.

Repent. . . . Save yourselves from this corrupt generation. [They] welcomed his message (cf. v. 38a, 40b, 41a).

What is it that the hearers are to do? In short, repent, that is to say, reverse direction in relation to the corruption of the old age. In this way, repentance is another key feature of the eschatological community. The generation or age, which with the coming of the Spirit instantly becomes old, is that of empire—in the case of the early community, the Roman Empire. Empire is known by oppression, injustice, violence. In short, empire is the way of death. Peter beckons the hearers to turn from and renounce these ways because now upon them is a new way, a new age centered on the risen Jesus and his way as Lord. So it is that even now in our churchly eschatological community, baptism involves us in renunciations of the ways of death that turn us from God and God's way.[85] With such repentance comes a welcome of the message about Jesus, a non-defensive receptivity to engagement with the new order of God's reign.

Be baptized every one of you… so that your sins may be forgiven, and you will receive the gift of the Holy Spirit (v. 38).

Initiation into the way of God's reign is through baptism. The Spirit's coming that births proclamation thus also gives birth to what would become the sacramental life of the church, baptism being a foundational rite for sharing fully in the life of the eschatological community. Baptism is inclusive in its wide embrace of "every one of you." It imparts the gift of forgiveness of sins, one of the qualities of life in the community of the new age known for its "second chances," as Walter notes in his work on the Holy Spirit.[86] So it is that confession and forgiveness, rooted ultimately in baptism, also will become one of the identified means of grace on which the church will center its life.[87] Baptism also imparts the gift of the Holy Spirit to the repentant hearers, the very same gift given to the Galileans who found themselves proclaiming in the languages of the nations.

They devoted themselves to the apostles' teaching and fellowship, to the breaking of bread and the prayers (v. 42).

Laid out here—"apostles' teaching, fellowship, breaking of bread, the prayers"—are elements central to the church's *ordo* for its life, central features of eschatological community through which we share in God's reign. So it has been through the centuries of this new age since Pentecost and its aftermath. I remember my sense of discovery upon encountering this verse from Acts in seminary, a discovery hidden in plain sight, that the current practice of the church has continuity through the centuries with the very beginnings of that first community.

Apostles' teaching involves focus on scripture, studied and proclaimed, as the teaching of the original apostles would eventually become Christian scripture. Fellowship—*koinonia*—is a quality of relating in Christian community that is consoling, life-giving, carrying Christ's presence when two are three are gathered together in his name.[88] Breaking of bread is a code phrase in Luke-Acts for what would become known as the eucharist, the eschatological meal that conveys the real presence of the risen Lord, for it is in the breaking of bread that he is recognized (Luke 24:30-31, 35). This meal is the eschatological banquet, a foretaste of the feast to come, another point that Walter makes in connecting the church with the messianic age.[89] The prayers may be code for the liturgical prayer of the community, rooted in the worship of the synagogue, centered on the Psalms, and perhaps also here a particular reference to the practice of intercessory prayer by which the church is known. These basic practices, it should be noted, are taken up with devotion: they *devoted* themselves to these things. It was thus not a matter of rote, mechanical participation.

Wonders and signs were being done by the apostles. All who believed were together and had all things in common; they would sell their possessions and goods and distribute the proceeds to all, as any had need (v. 43b-45).

A feature of apostolic ministry in the eschatological community includes wonders and signs. Acts certainly records such activity that we might name as miraculous. However, wonders and signs in a basic sense are common features of churchly life even today. For example, recipients of loving care and inspiration in the church may call it wonderful, significant, meaningful. A sign simply is that which is meaningful. En-Spirited meaning-making is thus also a feature of our life together in the new era.

Eschatological community is likewise known for its shared common life, its communal stewardship of goods and possessions. This social ministry is not just charity, but involves redistributive justice in the giving of such material benefits to those most in need. Such is the social ethic of God's reign manifest in the church, a radical freedom to be for others, a freedom made possible by the Spirit's coming. Such freedom of a Christian is central to Luther and also to Walter: "Only if you are fully free in the Spirit can you then be subject to others, and serve them truly."[90]

Day by day, as they spent much time together in the temple, they broke bread at home and ate their food (v. 46).

While the Pentecost event was an extraordinary moment in time, life in eschatological community is known for its daily-ness—life goes on *day by day*. So it has been for two millennia, still the extraordinary Spirit breaking into the ordinary routines of our life together. Moreover, the marking of time and participation in the church were and are not reduced to an hour on Sunday morning. Rather, the baptized "spent much time together." Life in eschatological community is time and labor intensive.

Life together in this community also had bi-locational moorings: temple and home. As there was as yet no church, as such, believers continued worship and participation in Hebrew traditions and practices. They were still Jewish after all, as Jesus was ever Jewish. We do well to mark, know, and inwardly digest this in our own day, recognizing our debt to our Jewish cousins in the faith. Domestic life was also a central feature of eschatological community and of the new age, as they broke bread also at home. So it is that centuries later, Luther's own rediscovery of the gospel and its practices would center bi-locationally on church and home. [91]

Awe came upon everyone . . . [and] with glad and generous hearts, praising God, [they had] the goodwill of all the people (v. 43a, 46b-47a).

Not only is the new age in eschatological community marked by particular activities—the *ordo* of churchly life—it is also characterized qualitatively by particular attitudes and dispositions: awe, glad and generous hearts, the praise of God or worshipfulness, the goodwill of all the people, a point to which Walter also attests.[92] It is thus not just *what* baptized believers of the new era do, but *how*, in what Spirit, they do what they do that is crucial. For such qualities themselves also proclaim the gospel, for we know from experience that manner of presence communicates content. A loving attitude communicates love. As was observed of the early Christians, "See how they love one another." Or as we have more recently known from a mid-twentieth century folk hymn, "They'll know we are Christians by our love." Life in eschatological community was and is, in short, awesome. Not only did features of the fruit of the Spirit (Galatians 5:22-23) have effects on the quality of life within in the community; it arguably inspired those around them, as the early members of the community evoked the goodwill of all the people.

The Promise is for you, for your children, and for all who are far away, everyone whom the Lord calls to him.... That day about three thousand persons were added (v. 39, 41b).

The promise rooted in the en-Spirited proclamation of the risen Jesus as Messiah and Lord was and is "for you, for your children, and for all who are far away." It is an inclusive promise, again, universal, catholic, another feature of eschatological community affirmed in Walter's work on the Holy Spirit.[93] Quite significantly, receptivity to this promise involves the initiative and beckoning of God—"those whom the Lord our God calls"—and so it is not so much a matter of personal and individual choice. Biblical pneumatology in Acts does not, therefore, center in on so-called "decision theology."

Yet another feature of this eschatological community is growth. Indeed, lives were turned upside down, transformed, and were marked by spiritual maturity and deepening. But the growth was also numerical: "That day about three thousand persons were added." Not a bad take for a day's proclamatory work! This growth continued day by day, numbers continuing to be added through the centuries until our own day of this era when the church numbers about two billion Christians in a world population of some seven billion people. Yet in biblical terms in Acts, numerical growth is not the stuff of "ecclesiastical obesity"—Walter's designation for the kind of crowded, superficial, and perhaps unhealthy expansion that can accompany versions of church growth movements.[94] Rather, growth is fundamentally spiritual, en-Spirited, rooted in the *ordo* of the church's life and proclamation, and known by qualities of presence that convey the fruit of the Spirit. Numerical growth is simply an organic by-product of such other features of growth and maturation. Or as St. Seraphim of Sarov would centuries later put it, writing about the quality of life once we receive the Holy Spirit: "Acquire inner peace and thousands around you will find their salvation."[95]

Summary and Conclusion

The Spirit's coming at Pentecost on the heels of Jesus' resurrection ushers in the eschatological age that unleashes proclamation of Jesus as Messiah and Lord, the effects of which then also birth the church—a community that is, as Walter puts it quoting Gerhard Lohfink, a "contrast society."[96] To what does this new community contrast? In the time of the Acts of the Apostles, it was the Roman Empire to which the emerging church as eschatological community contrasted. In our own age, as we remain in the eschatological last days, it is still empire expressed variously throughout the world today to which we in the church offer contrasting witness. As in the days of ancient Rome, so too today empire is about pluriform ways of death. The church as en-Spirited eschatological community is about the ways that make for life, made possible by the resurrection of Jesus, who is by virtue of that resurrection Lord, ruler, sovereign, the one who has the last word.

In particular, what Word of contrast do we see distilled from the preceding commentary on Acts 2, and, to some meaningful extent today, as lived and embodied by the church in fits and starts? Here is such a listing, suggested by Acts 2, of the ways of life in Christ which contrast with the imperial ways of death:

- Community over against individualism, the sound of the choir versus the solo voice.
- Unity, a unified witness even amidst cultural, ethnic, racial, national diversity—this in contrast to shrill voices of discord and divisive identity politics.
- A capacity to receive meaning *extra nos*, from outside of ourselves, transcending our sin-compromised innate capacities.
- A holistic approach to life versus silos, compartments, analytical reductionism that leaves parts strewn, de-constructed.
- Order in contrast to chaos.
- Intelligibility, not confusion.
- Giving voice to the voiceless, and inclusion and embrace for the marginalized in contrast to ways of exclusion and silencing of others.
- Commonwealth, in contrast to hoarding by elites, that nurtures a just distribution of God's abundance to all people.
- Authentic engagement with each other in a spirit of humility and compunction, in contrast to the multiplicity of arrogant defensive strategies we employ to disengage from others and even ourselves.
- Forgiveness, not punitive retribution and revenge.
- Genuine *koinonia*, community, and not just joining clubs of the like-minded.[97]

- Communal engagement day by day, and not just in individualized bubbles offering sound bytes, texts, Tweets going out pell-mell in the spirit of an epidemic of something like attention deficit disorder.
- Church participation in concert with meaningful domestic life, and not just shopping at the mall.
- Wonders, signs, awe, gladness, generosity, praise and worshipfulness, good will versus meaninglessness, fear, anger, mistrust, boredom, ennui, sadness, greed, cynicism, hopelessness, complaint, ill will.

In short, genuine life in eschatological community is marked by turning from the various ways of death to these multiple dimensions of the way of life, for such life has the last word because the risen Jesus *is* that last Word. Such eschatological community is marked also by growth, not decline. Indeed, I trust that churches which live robustly in the Spirit in the above-listed ways will, naturally and organically, grow by attraction without programs and gimmicks.

These qualities of eschatological, ecclesial communal life are matters of life and death today as they always have been. In this season of the world's age as I write in dialogue with Walter and his theology, our nation is torn yet again by racial and socio-economic divides that seem to be ever widening. The world's human population has doubled in my half-century lifetime, accelerating competition for resources seemingly ever more scarce. Climate change, arguably a symptom and outcome of this fevered pitch approach to living, may be ushering in an ultimate age of death, what some are calling the anthropocene extinction event. In short, our human ways of death have metastasized. Our very earth and its ecosystems have a fever, and our island home would heal herself through climatic upheaval and re-ordering. May the church as eschatological community in its life and witness to the risen Jesus as Messiah and Lord, and firmly rooted in the means of grace, be a healing, saving antidote for the nations and for the cosmos.

The summary listing of the qualities of life in the church as "contrast society" constitutes our protest marching orders for the sake of the world. Likewise, this listing of the features of life in eschatological community sets the agenda for the church's mission to proclaim Christ in word and deed. The *ordo* of the new order of the reign of God is ours to live and witness to in the power of the Holy Spirit. Indeed, when the church proclaims Jesus as Lord via its actions in living according to Christ's ways of life, this is also the Holy Spirit! In the risen Christ and with the Spirit's coming, we have been given the radically gracious gift, the down payment on the consummated reign of God that allows us to begin to live this sacred reality even now. May God in Christ, through the power of the Holy Spirit, use us, Christ's body, the church, to continue to turn the world and its logic upside down. Thus, may the Spirit turn up the heat to cool things down for God's reign of shalom, peace, commonwealth, holistic well-being for all of creation.

All of Life Is Sacramental
A New Way of Being and Seeing

Michael Rinehart

The sacraments invite us into a new way of seeing the world and a new way of being in the world. They invite us to *see* the world sacramentally and to *live* sacramentally. When we do, all of life starts to become sacramental, from the kiss of a loved one to the kindness of a stranger.

How many sacraments are there? Are there seven sacraments or two?

It might come as a surprise that some early Christians believed there were more than two or even seven sacraments. While it may be relatively simple to decide how many "chief rites" the church has, depending on a particular sacramental theology, it is not quite so easy to distinguish which what aspects of life most unambiguously reflect the divine.

In his lectures to aspiring pastors and others across the church, Walter Bouman referred to the sacraments as "the means of grace." The law brings judgment; the gospel brings grace. The sacraments are those vehicles or signs that bear God's message of grace to us. So the question might then be, "How many signposts of grace are there in this world?" We begin by asking, "What is a sacrament?"

What Is a Sacrament?

If we could ask the apostles how many "sacraments" there were, they would likely consider our question absurd. The Latin word for "sacrament" corresponds to the Greek word for "mystery," so asking them how many mysteries there were might elicit a perplexed stare.

The eventual use of the word sacrament as a rite of the church would come along much later. Augustine (354-430) said that a sacrament was a visible word,[98] an outward sign of an inward grace. He would number them differently than Catholics or Protestants today, however, for he considered the Nicene Creed and Lord's Prayer to be sacraments.

John of Damascus (676-749) said there were two. Peter Damien (1007-1072) said there were twelve sacraments. Some considered the consecration of a king or queen a sacrament. Over time, the word sacrament came to be understood as a chief liturgical ritual of the church, commanded or instituted by Christ, which conferred grace using some outward sign. The number was set at seven by the thirteenth century, just as there were seven angels or seven churches in John's Apocalypse. Thomas Aquinas (1225-1274) further developed an understanding of the sacraments in his scholastic theology. He understood a sacrament to require three things: an outward sign, an inward grace, and divine institution.

Reformers Martin Luther (1483-1546) and Philipp Melanchthon (1497-1560) began with Aquinas's understanding. The Apology to the Augsburg Confession, authored by Melanchthon, defines the sacraments as "rites which have the command of God, and to which the promise of grace has been added." It lists Baptism, the Lord's Supper, and Absolution as "true sacraments." Three.

The Apology makes clear that confirmation and extreme unction (last rites) have no command in Scripture, and therefore cannot be considered sacraments.[99] Likewise, confirmation is a human tradition with no basis in Scripture or the early church. Elsewhere Luther jokes that perhaps the sacrament of confirmation was invented to embellish the duties of bishops lest they be without function in the church.[100] The question is raised in the Apology, however, whether or not prayer and almsgiving might be considered sacraments, since both are commanded by our Lord.

What of marriage, however? Is marriage not instituted by God in Genesis? Are we not told that a man shall leave his mother and cleave to his wife? Are we not commanded to be fruitful and multiply? Might not the marriage ring be understood as an outward sign of the inward grace? Does Ephesians not refer to the union of husband and wife as a "mystery"? Nevertheless, the reformers would conclude that since Christ never commanded marriage, it cannot be a sacrament.

What of anointing? Are we not commanded in the New Testament to lay hands on the sick in prayer and anoint them with oil? Is oil not a physical element, an outward sign? What about foot washing? Luther asks. How many commands of Christ are there in the gospels? Shall we make sacraments of all of them?

In *The Babylonian Captivity of the Church*, Luther wonders about preaching: "But if everything the apostles did is a sacrament, why have they not rather made preaching a sacrament?"[101] After 1520, he reduced the number of sacraments from three to two. Absolution has no physical element (outward sign), and is, at its foundation, an outgrowth of baptism in his view.

Later, after struggling with these questions at length, Melanchthon concluded that arguing over the number of sacraments was a ridiculous endeavor. It is hard to imagine what good can come out of such an argument. It seems that such things belong to the era of Scholastic theology, along with arguing about how many angels can dance on the head of a pin. It would be fortunate if our ecumenical dialogues today would not get hung up on this matter. When speaking of the mysteries, we need an air of humility.

Luther points out[102] that Christ himself is called a sacrament in 1 Timothy 3:16:

> Without any doubt, the mystery of our religion is great:
> He was revealed in flesh,
> vindicated in spirit,
> seen by angels,
> proclaimed among Gentiles,
> believed in throughout the world,
> taken up in glory.

Luther muses that if Christ himself is a sacrament, why don't we have an eighth sacrament?[103]

While the Orthodox Church recognizes the seven Roman Catholic sacraments, it has never strictly defined a limited number of sacraments. It also recognizes these as sacramental rites: burial of the dead, rites for a monastic profession, blessing of waters at Epiphany, and the anointing of a monarch.

Can we limit the mysteries of faith and life? We can argue about how many official church rituals there are, but does such an argument embody the mysteries of the faith? Perhaps we would do well to step back and cast a wider net. Can we recapture a sense of the sacred mystery that sacraments are meant to convey?

Many things in life are sacramental. They point to realities and sacred truths beyond the facade of our daily existence. The universe is a wonderful and mysterious place, and there is more to life than meets the eye. In this we begin to see a broader definition of a sacrament as "something regarded as possessing a sacred character or mysterious significance."[104] Much in life conveys a sense of the sacred, that which is holy. What outward, physical elements reveal the underlying, profound realities of life?

Let's look at sacraments from another angle.

The Sacraments Reveal the Mystery of Life, Death, and Resurrection

On the evening of the resurrection, two disciples encounter a stranger as they are walking to Emmaus. They do not recognize him, but hearers of Luke 24:13–35 learn that this is Jesus himself. The divine is often disguised in the trappings of the mundane. After a revealing conversation that gets their hearts beating, they arrive at their destination. At their invitation, he agrees to stay with them for dinner. The moment he breaks the bread their eyes are opened, and they recognize him.

The simple acts of walking, talking, and breaking bread together become a vehicle that gives these two disciples a glimpse beyond this world in which we live. Word and meal become sacramental. The stranger on the road opens the Scriptures, which consistently point to an otherworldly eschatological reality beyond the existential reality in which we live. "On this mountain the Lord will prepare a feast . . . and he will destroy death forever" (Isaiah 25:6-8a).

The disciples catch the vision that Jesus' death on the cross is linked to his presence with them. In that moment are hints of that which is to come. They can begin to imagine what they cannot see. In the breaking of the bread, he was made known to them—but not just him. God's future is revealed, uncovered in the meal! This is the nature of sacraments. They are ordinary things that reveal extraordinary realities.

In his lectures, Bouman recognized that revelation comes in many forms in addition to Word and Sacrament. God is revealed in the stars, in every flower of the field, in the sacrificial love of a stranger, and in myriad other ways. The apostle Paul also points this out in his letter to the Romans: "Ever since the creation of the world his eternal power and divine nature, invisible though they are, have been understood and seen through the things he has made" (Romans 1:20).

Paul recognized that the hidden God was revealed in nature. As the moon reflects the light of the sun, so nature reflects the light of its Creator. Even persons whom Paul considered "ungodly" recognized that the things that God has made reflect the invisible, eternal powers and divine nature of the hand that made them. The scriptures are revelation. The sacraments are revelation. God reveals God's true nature in many ways. The spiritual is revealed in the physical. Put more simply, the invisible is revealed in that which is visible. Spiritual things are those that cannot be seen.

When asked what we mean by "spiritual," we might point to intangible fruits of the spirit in Galatians 5:22: love, joy, peace, patience, and so on. They cannot be seen. They cannot be touched, tasted, smelled, heard, or examined in a test tube, and yet they are some of the most important realities of our lives. A sacrament is something tangible that gives evidence to something intangible.

How do we know that there is love? Love becomes real for people when it becomes incarnate in the form of a hug, a gift, a gesture.

Everything we do, everything we say is sacramental. Every action, every gesture, is evidence of some deeper invisible, intangible reality. Our lives are sacramental. The giving of bread in Holy Communion is a sacramental act, but so is the giving of bread to a beggar on the street. The act of generosity points to something beyond itself—compassion, or the truth that something matters beyond our own survival and well-being.

If we cannot see the sacred nature of a simple act like sharing bread with someone in need, it is not likely that we will see the sacred nature of the sharing of bread in worship. The principle of sacramentality recognizes that there is more to life than meets the eye—that we have faith to see that there is more to the universe than what we can touch, smell, or hear.

For the sacraments to have any value to us, we must be open to an awareness of the divine. Perhaps this is a post-Enlightenment way to understand the medieval argument of whether faith was necessary to benefit from the sacraments or whether they were efficacious *ex opere operato*. Some felt that the sacraments conferred gifts of grace regardless of the attitude of the recipient or simply by being in the room when the bread was consecrated.

The Reformers disagreed: "Thus we teach that in using the sacraments there must be a faith which believes these promises and accepts that which is promised and offered in the sacrament."[105]

A sacrament is a physical promise of a spiritual reality. Faith is the attitude of openness that accepts the gift that is promised. Perhaps this is why Jesus encouraged his followers to have the faith of a child. Such faith is a posture of openness to the world, even aspects of the world we cannot see or comprehend.

How we see the world matters. One person may view the sharing of bread as a handout to an unworthy charlatan, while the other may see it as an act of compassion. One may view a sunrise as a miraculous moment, while another sees it as the start of another day of drudgery heralded by a burning ball of gas about to explode.

There is a paradox here. We need faith for the sacraments to be efficacious, and yet one of the gifts of the sacraments is that they awaken faith. They are a means of grace. They awaken faith and point to the deeper truths and mysteries of life.

The Augsburg Confession says that the sacraments are "instituted to awaken and confirm faith in those who use them." For Bouman as for Luther, faith is trust in God's promises. Therefore, the sacraments are those outward signs commanded by God that promise grace and awaken our trust of God and God's promises. The author of Hebrews puts it this way: "Now faith is the assurance of things hoped for, the conviction of things not seen" (Hebrews 11:1). The sacraments reinforce this faith.

Faith is not intellectual assent to doctrines or creeds, but rather putting all of our trust in God. Faith is trusting the God who in Christ's crucifixion sides with the innocent, the suffering and vulnerable and, in Christ's resurrection, promises eternal life. Bouman proclaimed this understanding of faith vigorously in every lecture, in every sermon, and even on his deathbed. Faith is not believing "six impossible things before breakfast," as the White Queen said she was able to do in Lewis Carroll's *Through the Looking Glass.* Nor is faith belief in facts. Faith is, as Paul Tillich said, "ultimate trust." Faith is the child who jumps off of the kitchen counter into her father's arms, understanding little but trusting completely.

Faith is placing our trust in the Source of Life, who is revealed most profoundly in the life, death, and resurrection of Jesus of Nazareth, the crucified Jew. This faith frees us from our bondage to other gods that vie for our allegiance and enslave us. They promise much but deliver little.

By contrast, when we say, "I believe Jesus is Lord," we proclaim that Jesus' way of being in the world is my way of being in the world. This was essentially Bouman's theology and soteriology. Confessing Christ as Lord saves us from in the need to justify ourselves or to serve other gods of wealth, power, or state. The Word and the sacraments as the visible Word awaken this faith/trust within us.

But that which awakens faith is not limited to two, three or even seven liturgical rites if it is possible that a flower might be sacramental, or that a bird might stir and awaken faith. Consider Jesus' words from the Sermon on the Mount:

> Look at the birds of the air; they neither sow nor reap nor gather into barns, and yet your heavenly Father feeds them. Are you not of more value than they? And can any of you by worrying add a single hour to your span of life? And why do you worry about clothing? Consider the lilies of the field, how they grow; they neither toil nor spin, yet I tell you, even Solomon in all his glory was not clothed like one of these. But if God so clothes the grass of the field, which is alive today and tomorrow is thrown into the oven, will he not much more clothe you—you of little faith? . . . But strive first for the kingdom of God and his righteousness, and all these things will be given to you as well (Matthew 6:26-30, 33).

Jesus did not grow up in the big city of Jerusalem, but rather in Galilee, in a small town, so small that it's not even mentioned in the Hebrew Bible. It is not hard to imagine Jesus and his disciples wading through some Galilean field, watching the birds and brushing the flowers with their hands. "Have faith," Jesus says. "God takes care of the birds. Don't you imagine God will also provide for you?"

It may be natural to seek tangible needs like food, clothing, and shelter first, before seeking less tangible things like love, belonging, and what Maslow calls "self-actualization." But if we seek only the tangible, we may never get beyond them to the higher, intangible, spiritual things. Jesus teaches anyone who will listen to see the spiritual things first.

Furthermore, he teaches people to see the tangible things as gateways to the spiritual. Water becomes wine. For Nicodemus physical rebirth is a metaphor for spiritual rebirth. The blind receiving their sight is about learning to see the world with spiritual eyes. The thirst-quenching water drawn by the woman at the well is second to Jesus' living water that quenches our spiritual thirst. The bread at the feeding of the multitude prefigures the bread of life that feeds our souls. For Jesus, all of life is sacramental. Everything physical points to the spiritual. Things *seen* draw us to things *un*seen.

Until we grasp this sacramental view of life, the so-called sacraments, however many of them there may be, will be only rituals for an institutional church. Until we open our hearts to the possibility of mysteries that we cannot begin to comprehend, to realities of the universe that we are too limited to see, we will miss that to which the sacraments point. Faith receives the gifts promised. The proper preface for Christmas poetically strives to convey this:

> In the wonder and mystery of the Word made flesh you have opened the eyes of faith to a new and radiant vision of your glory, that beholding the God made visible, we may be drawn to love the God whom we cannot see.[106]

Here Christ himself is seen as sacramental: Jesus is the primary sacrament.

The Chief Sacraments

A discussion of the chief sacraments draws us back to the traditional seven sacraments. In Volume 2 of his systematic theology, *Jesus is Risen: Theology for the Church*,[107] Bouman rightly spends the majority of his time elaborating on the two chief sacraments of the church: baptism and communion. Seeing life sacramentally is critical, but even if we consent that all of life is sacramental, pointing beyond what we see to truths we cannot see, we would also have to agree that not all sacraments are equal. Birds, flowers, and the like may point us to the truth of God's providence and awaken us to a deeper trust in God for the tangible needs of this life—so that we may spend more energy looking for the intangible things of life—but they don't necessarily point us to the eschatological truth that death does not have the final word.

While Catholics and Episcopalians profess seven sacraments, both speak of two chief or principal sacraments: baptism and communion.

This has been affirmed for hundreds of years. Albertus Magnus (1193-1280) is said to have stated, "... the Church was formed from the side of the dying and dead Christ, as the two chief sacraments poured from his side—the blood of redemption and the water of absolution."

The chief sacraments of the church draw us to the specific ministry of death and resurrection as seen in Christ. Once we see all of life as sacramental, the chief sacraments take on heightened meaning. They focus us on Christ as the ultimate sacrament, and they ground sacramental thinking in weekly event. Rather than waiting to stumble upon sacramental signs that point us beyond this life, weekly communion and remembrance of baptism draw us regularly and rhythmically into the mystical drama of life and death, lest we lose sight of spiritual things. Just as the initiation of circumcision and the meal of Passover came to define the Jewish faith and devotion to the law, so the initiation of baptism and the meal of communion meal came to define the Christian faith and devotion to the gospel.

Bouman describes baptism as a ritual initiation into the eschatological community. "The Holy Spirit is the down payment (Ephesians 1:14; 2 Corinthians 5:5) on the coming consummation of the Messianic Age, so the Spirit is prayed for and conferred through the laying-on-of-hands and chrismation (blessing) with oil. This makes unmistakable the eschatological character of Baptism."[108]

"The meal," Bouman says, is "connected to future salvation in Isaiah 25:6-9, which begins, 'On this mountain the Lord of hosts will make for all peoples a feast of rich food, a feast of well-aged wines, of rich food filled with marrow, of well-aged wines strained clear. And he will destroy on this mountain the shroud that is cast over all peoples, the sheet that is spread over all nations; he will swallow up death forever.'"

In both baptism and holy communion we are drawn quite specifically into an intangible reality we cannot currently see or intellectually grasp—the kingdom of God, the messianic age, where death is swallowed up forever. Both are outward signs of an inward grace. Both have the command of Christ ("Go therefore and make disciples of all nations, baptizing them in the name of the Father and the Son and of the Holy Spirit. . . ." and "Do this in remembrance of me"), and both offer the promise of eternal life.

Participation in these sacraments does more than give us a mere glimpse of the future, "a foretaste of the feast to come." It invites us to see all of life sacramentally and to be about the risky business of participating in that future now, whatever the cost. They invite us to be sacraments of God's grace. They invite us to see our lives as visible signs of grace, signs that point to spiritual realities that are hard to grasp when we are focused on the material things of life. As Bouman says, when we share in this meal, "something happens." We become what we eat: the body of Christ for the world.

All of Life is Sacramental

None of this is magic. There is no hocus-pocus here, a word which ironically derived from the eucharistic liturgy: *Hoc est (enim) corpus (meum)*, "This is my body." The sacrament of holy communion is not a primitive incantation for a pre-modern ceremony. It is rather a ritual meal like Passover or Thanksgiving, which points beyond itself, draws us into a new way of seeing and being.

This is instead participation in a meal that gives us a new way of seeing and being. Baptism is initiation into this new, sacramental way of seeing and being.

When Jesus had his last supper with the disciples and said the words, "Do this in remembrance of me," he invited them not just to remember him whenever they subsequently broke bread together, like friends at a wake, but to remember his way of seeing the world and participate in his way of being in the world. Because death does not have the final word, I am free to live joyfully, love freely, give generously, and be a sign of God's kingdom. Like the early church, we gather around bread and wine to take part in a messianic meal that invites us to see God's future for humanity, a future that cannot be seen with our physical eyes, but only through the eyes of faith. We leave that gathering encouraged to see the world sacramentally, to live sacramentally. We are sent into the world to recklessly live the vision we are given, as living sacraments ourselves, eyes wide opened to the mysteries of the universe.

Walter Bouman
A Reflection

John Buchanan

I think about Walter Bouman a lot, but particularly on the first Sunday of Advent every three years, when Isaiah 64:1-9 shows up in the lectionary:

> Oh that you would tear open the heavens and come down,
> so that the mountains would quake at your presence—
> to make your name known to your adversaries.

Walt preached on that text once, and one of his students who happened to be on the staff of the church I was serving at the time, Broad Street Presbyterian Church of Columbus, Ohio, gave me a copy. "I think you're going to like this," she said, and I did. In fact, it is the best, most winsome Advent sermon I ever read or heard, and I have been using it shamelessly for thirty years. I am always careful to attribute it to Walt and make him part of my sermon, which is easy to do. Walt began his sermon by referring the congregation to a contemporary literary resource with profound theological meaning, by sharing his favorites from *Children's Letters to God:*[109]

Dear God,

Are you really invisible or is it just a trick?

Lucy

Dear God,

Thank you for the baby brother, but what I prayed for was a puppy.

Joyce

Dear God,

Maybe Cain and Abel would not kill each other if they had their own rooms. It works with my brother.

Larry

Walt said his favorite was a profound Advent prayer:

Dear God,

Are you real? Some people don't believe it. If you are, you better do something quick.

Harriet Anne

It is the oldest prayer in history. It was surely prayed by the exile community living in Babylonian captivity, trying to make sense of what had happened to them. Their humiliating situation called into question everything they had been taught and believed about their chosenness. The defeat of their army, the destruction of their holy city, and, most of all, the devastation of the temple, the heart of their identity as God's people, prompted some of the most poignant poetry:

> By the rivers of Babylon—
> there we sat down and there we wept
> when we remembered Zion. . . .
> On the willows there
> we hung up our harps.
> For there our captors
> asked us for song,
> and our tormentors asked for mirth, saying
> "Sing us one of the songs of Zion!"
> How could we sing the Lord's song
> in a foreign land? (Psalm 137)

Paraphrasing Second Isaiah, Harriet Anne prayed a prayer people have been praying since the beginning of time: "Dear God . . . you better do something quick."

Walter Bouman's deep, luminous faith, grounded in God's grace and the incarnation, Word become flesh, informed his compelling Advent proclamation that God, indeed, has done something in human history. It was not the dramatic tearing open of the heavens that the prophet asked for. Rather, it was the birth of a child, Emmanuel, God with us.

And so, I remember Walt every time I ponder the mysterious, provocative message of Advent: that God has come and does come and continues to come into the life of the world to reconcile and redeem and save. And every year as I experience the warm, joyful anticipation of Advent, I find that I am left, finally, with the reality Walter Bouman understood and advocated for and personally lived—the church of Jesus Christ, the body of the incarnation, the community through which God chooses to continue the long, irresistible process of saving the world. The church!

He was a great churchman, a big, robust Lutheran with a sweet spirit and a winsome worldliness that would have made Luther himself proud. He was, quite simply, the best teacher I ever experienced, with an uncanny ability to convey intricate, complex ideas in ways people could understand. His sense of humor helped, of course, as did his understanding of the issues confronting the world. People responded not only to his obvious erudition but his authentic, energetic humanity was well. We invited him regularly to teach in the adult education program at Broad Street Presbyterian, and he was an all-time favorite. Every time we advertised a presentation by Professor Walter Bouman we knew we would need to set up extra chairs in the hall. A prominent Columbus orthopedic surgeon and a church member both remember that Walter was a mesmerizing teacher, that the hall was packed whenever he taught, and that he always began with a story or two, always very funny but with an appropriate entry to the topic of the day. During pastoral transitions Walter preached from the

Presbyterian pulpit and on one occasion the church's adult education committee proposed that honorary Presbyterian membership be extended to him.

The surgeon, J. Richard Briggs, and his wife, Marilyn, became friends with Walter and Jan, and when Walt became ill, visited him both in the hospital and at home. Dick recalled his last visit with Walter just two days before he died. The hospice nurse and Jan were in the room during the visit. The conversation was not easy; Walter was not very responsive. But suddenly, when Dick asked a question, Walter became alert, fully responsive, and fully conversational, launching into what Dick remembers as a fifteen-minute elegant description of Christian faith. Dick said he was privileged to hear Walter's final theology lecture delivered from the bed in which he would die in forty-eight hours.

Walter had a big theology and an equally big ecclesiology. Ecumenism came naturally to him and grew out of his deep sense of the wideness of God's mercy and the unconditional gift of God's grace.

I will not add here to the current ecclesiastical hand-wringing and obsessive analysis over the crisis of the church in our day, particularly the mainline Protestant church. Lutherans are not always included in the literature about the mainline. But Walter Bouman spent enough time in a Presbyterian church and other congregations to qualify as a card-carrying mainliner. In regard to the mainline situation, I particularly like Phyllis Tickle's "Rummage Sale" metaphor.[110] Every 500 years or so, she proposes, the church undergoes the ecclesiastical equivalent of a rummage sale. Old, worn-out, obsolete stuff is discarded and moved out in order to make room for new stuff. Beginning before the Common Era, every 500 years major change happens. There is some kind of major shift, a break from the mainstream that at the time is experienced as tragic. In fact, what has happened at half-millennial intervals is that a new structure emerges. In response, the old structure renews and reforms itself and the two move, on parallel tracks, into the future. It has happened twice in the last millennium: the split between the Eastern and Western church and emergence of Eastern

Orthodoxy; and, 500 years later, the Reformation and the emergence of Protestantism and Counter-Reformation Roman Catholicism. If Tickle is even close to correct, and I believe she is, we are in the midst of an ecclesiastical Rummage Sale, and it is not clear yet what exactly will emerge from it. There are hints—in the Emergent Church Movement, the Presbyterian 1001 Worshipping Communities project of the PC(USA), and other often ecumenical initiatives.

Whatever new form of church is born will be incarnational in terms of its love for and deep involvement in the life of the world. It will not be much interested in the old denominational identities but committed to the oneness of all believers. It will be inter-faith in terms of its openness to the world's amazing racial, ethnic, and religious diversity, grateful for the religious tradition and practices of all the world's people.

I think I see a hint of what is coming in the family of one of my adult children. He is a Presbyterian. She is a Roman Catholic. Their three daughters attend a Catholic parochial school, and they attend the parish church when they are not in Sunday school and worship at the Presbyterian Church. They were baptized in the Presbyterian Church and had their first communion in their Catholic Church, a wonderful liturgical celebration in which I participated at the invitation of the parish priest. I don't know how many ecclesiastical rules were broken when I gave the bread to my granddaughter, kneeling with fifty other third graders and said, "Lilly, the Body of Christ broken for you," but I was profoundly grateful. They don't know and don't seem to care about all the historic reasons Roman Catholics and Protestants have found not to worship together, have argued and demeaned when they weren't fighting and killing one another. The three of them exhibit a wonderful, grace-filled, post-Roman Catholic/Protestant Christianity, a church truly "catholic," like the one Jimmy Breslin described when he said about any church that calls itself catholic: "Here comes everybody."

Two of our families are impatient with their church because, until recently, it was not very welcoming to a daughter and sister because of sexual orientation. When my adult children heard that I was off to another meeting to talk about sexual orientation, they used to say, in unison, "Dad, are you still talking about that? Don't you know that the world has moved on? It's not an issue anywhere else anymore."

Robert Putnam and David Campbell in *American Grace: How Religion Unites and Divides Us*,[111] confirms their sentiment. Young adults, Putnam and Campbell argue, leave churches and become part of the "nones," i.e. people who answer "none" to pollsters' questions about religious preference, because of what they are hearing and seeing about religion in the media: harsh, self-confident to the point of arrogance, exclusivist, trivial, negative and judgmental about sexual issues particularly sexual orientation, and downright mean.

Whatever church emerges out of this Rummage Sale will have gotten past the public battle over "hot-button" issues and will be as shockingly open to the world and as radically inclusive as its Lord was. The church that emerges will be radically open to other religious tradition, a lot less obsessive about guarding its traditions and getting its rules and doctrines right than it is about getting Jesus right when he sat down at table and broke bread and drank wine with all sorts of people, particularly those who were regarded as unfit and unclean.

And, I pray that whatever church emerges will take its essential, Christ-centered unity half as seriously as he did. It will be a church that remembers and, in its practices, expresses some of his last words: "Protect them, holy Father, that they may be one, as we are one. . . . that they may all be one so that the world may believe you have sent me" (John 17:11, 20). According to Jesus, ecumenism is anything but a liberal agenda. Rather it is central to the evangelical mandate: "By this everyone will know that you are my disciples, if you have love for one another" (John 13:34).

The new ecumenical frontier will be interfaith. Hans Kung famously said that there will be no peace among nations until there is peace among religions, and there will be no peace among religions until there is dialogue among religions. The future calls the church to a new openness. The urgent demands of peace call the church of Jesus Christ to an acknowledgement of truth larger than anyone's particular truth.

University of Chicago Professor of Modern Jewish History and Thought Paul Mendes-Flohr reminds all people of faith that we are called to something beyond tolerance, that Goethe said, "To tolerate is to insult—tolerance is not far from indifference." We must now acknowledge that within any monotheism there is a tendency toward intolerance and worse. The challenge before all people and communities of faith, Mendes-Flohr argues, is to maintain "fidelity to the theological positions and values of one's own religious community, while acknowledging the cognitive and spiritual integrity of other faith communities."[112]

In the midst of appalling violence, if not between religions, at least perpetrated by extremist adherents of one religion or another, it is clear that we really must stop the old tradition of trying to eliminate one another by conversion or persecution or death. Mendes-Flohr calls for "dialogical tolerance," a path of mutual acknowledgment and understanding, without compromising one's own faith commitment.

The church that emerges in the future will be grounded in something more than those creeds and doctrines and dogma that so frequently have been barriers that divide, something more than revelation as a disclosure of intellectual truth, but rather a disclosure of Divine presence. The church that emerges will represent a religion that seeks and trusts the mysterious sacred among us all. It will understand that Jesus Christ came into the world not to give us better beliefs but God's presence, God's essence, God's love.

We can't even begin to talk about that until we get our own unity right, "that they may be one so that the world might believe."

Is there a more urgent priority and more poignant pleas than this, written 2,000 years ago from a prison cell? "I, therefore, a prisoner in the Lord, beg you to lead a life worthy of the calling to which you were called, with all humility and gentleness, with patience, bearing with one another in love, making every effort to maintain the unity of the spirit in the bond of peace" (Ephesians 4: 1-3).

It is a singular moment. Sitting in a filthy jail cell, Paul has a vision of a new humanity God has created in which old divisions are healed, walls of hostility are broken down, and all things are reconciled and united.

Distinguished New Testament scholar Marcus Barth used to say that "Make every effort to maintain unity" is much too mild. The Greek, Barth said, is urgent, passionate, a full intellectual, spiritual, and physical effort. "Do it! Do it now! Do whatever it takes to get it done."

Walter Bouman, in his teaching ministry and in his life, honored that magnificent and urgent hope, for the Holy Catholic Church and for the world and the whole creation.

Walter's friendship was a precious gift. His warmth and laughter, his deep faith and profound understanding, deepened my own faith and stretched my vision. His genuine love for God and devotion to the church of Jesus Chris, and his obvious joy in the Resurrection enriched my life.

Thanks be to God.

Quintessentially Walter Bouman

J. Robert Wright

The invitation for me to contribute an essay in the volume to honor the late Walter Bouman leads me to offer these following memories in recollection of a valued friend, dedicated ecumenist, and perceptive scholar whom I held in very high regard.

I want to record one particular insight about Walter which, in a very real way, sums up my esteem of him and requires no quotation marks, but which will probably be immediately recognized as "quintessentially Walter Bouman." It is a very brief remark that I heard him make more than once, especially in the context of sermons he was preaching, and it constitutes in its own way his own summary of the Christian gospel to which he and his gracious wife were so firmly committed.

Walter said, and said more than once, that in reading any novel, or other book or anything else (such as a portion of the Bible, for instance), he always preferred to begin at its end—to read first how it would turn out at its conclusion. This approach could and indeed would almost always give him the insight he wanted and needed as to what that particular author wanted to tell his or her readers about the core or essence of the gospel. This is "his message" that I always take from him.

Now, when I first heard Walter say this, or something similar, I paused to collect my thoughts, for this is not the way I was accustomed to reading books. I was trained in the Oxford school of history, where names and dates and spelling and references and footnotes and academic precision are all important. I did not really agree with that approach, but neither did I fully want to reject it. So what did I conclude?

Perhaps in good Anglican fashion, over the following years, I have reached more of a "both . . . and" approach. From some kinds of books I look for some sort of edification and from others I expect a different kind of precision. In my own writing, I sometimes follow the former style, and sometimes the latter. Usually I believe that there can be "different strokes for different folks," as Walter might say, and I am grateful to him for leading me to be a bit more flexible in this regard. Indeed, this very essay is an example of my willingness to admit—and even tolerate—such a technique. Of course, I am certain that I have not been entirely converted to what I believe was the approach that Walter usually seemed to prefer, but I do give much thanks for his life and teaching.

PART III
Alleluia!

Trinity
Why "Abba"?

Becky Robbins-Penniman

Foreword

This paper on the theology of the Trinity was written as an assignment for Systematic Theology I, which I took from Walter Bouman in 1996 at Trinity Lutheran Seminary. Walt liked the paper a lot; in fact, he asked for a copy. Actually, he did that often with students and had file cabinets stuffed with papers from his decades of teaching. I learned of his practice after becoming a teaching assistant for the History/Theology/Society Division at the seminary and began working closely with Walt and the other exceptional professors who shaped, challenged, and delighted me. The five wonderful years I spent in seminary (I attended part-time) were the most intellectually stimulating years of my life—far more so than my studies and practice in law, which was my first career.

I have now been a parish pastor for fifteen years. Now and then over that time, I came across this paper on the theology of the Trinity, usually when moving offices and my own stuffed file cabinets. I pulled it out again when this *Gedenkschrift* honoring Walt was announced and I was invited to submit an essay in his honor. On the one hand, I would do almost anything in my power to honor my beloved mentor. On the other, I have not done any academic writing since being handed my seminary diploma, nor do I have access to scholarly reference materials in the quaint seaside community in Florida where I live and serve. I simply could not offer anything new to the volume of an academic or scholarly caliber. I can say honestly, however, that my theology has not changed much in the intervening years, and I still work within the framework described in this paper day in and day out; even now, it shapes my sermons, pastoral approach, and prayer life. Nancy Raabe and Ann Haut thought including a paper Walt had liked would be an acceptable offering. Thus, although I have updated the graphics and added this foreword and the last section on the implications of my paper, the main body is pretty much as I submitted it nearly eighteen years ago.

Introduction

Feminist theologians and even sensitive churchgoers have expressed discomfort with the witness in the Gospel of Mark that Jesus used the endearment of "Daddy" to address God during Jesus' agonized prayer in Gethsemane (see Mark 14:36). Besides the intimate term "Abba," Jesus often referred to God as "Father." As one of the bases for the assertion through the ages that this indicated some primacy of maleness, the gendered references have been an increasingly discordant factor in the development of Christianity.

The response by some has been to give up on the Trinity as hopelessly sexist and oppressive, and to refuse to use the traditional trinitarian references to God.[113] Some try to ignore the biblical witness and substitute other names, metaphors, or even the functions of God, whenever God as "Father" is mentioned (e.g., "Creator, Redeemer, Sanctifier").[114] Others have added on female titles, such as "Mother," whenever "Father" is used.[115] Finally, another tactic has been to admit to "Father," but then assert the femininity of the Spirit, to balance things out a little, even though this retains a male predominance of two against one.[116] Of course, the vast majority simply live with the scriptural description and its cultural consequences; feminist and sensitive attitudes range from resignation to confusion to barely tolerable exasperation.

Another approach is possible. This approach accepts the biblical witness, but rejects the correlative assertion that by calling God "Father," Jesus was thereby setting human males up as being so much "like God" that they are privileged and thus "lord" over those who are not male. This alternate approach requires that we look at the very essence of what the word "father" might signify from a *transactional*, rather than *cultural*, perspective.

Theology from Below

Making theological excursions into the nature of God is always a dicey business. With seemingly unshakable confidence (but more likely bravado), mere mortals make postulations about who, what, and how God is. When this happens, we need to pay close attention as to how conclusions about the nature of the ineffable Godhead have been grounded and supported.

When humans assert that they *know* something, they are stating that they understand something, that it has some kind of meaning for them. "Knowledge" based on speculation about the nature of something—in this case, God—is typically grounded in claims of revelation. Challenges to such conclusions usually are met with appeals to special insight, the mystery of God, or the statements of prior luminaries who have been accorded authoritative status by the relevant community.

To avoid speculative conclusions, our thinking must be grounded in that which we know based on observation and experience. We may be wrong about the facts or events that we think we have observed or experienced, but we should be able at least to articulate a rationale for our conclusions that is founded on information available and meaningful not only to us, but also to our audience. Under this alternative, even a seemingly revelatory, out-of-the-blue notion about God must be consistent with, and grounded in, that which humans in general are able to observe or experience.

In christology from below, we ground our conclusions about God by looking at the witness and experience of the life, death, and resurrection of Jesus the Christ. In this, we are looking at God as the One who saves. Similarly, in trying to make additional determinations about God, it is legitimate to look at the actions of God as the One who creates, as this is one of the acknowledged functions of God. Just as aspects about a painter may be known through the artist's canvasses, or information about a musician may be gleaned from various compositions, so can we gain information about the Creator by looking at creation.

To be coherent, "knowledge," that which is said about the One who creates must be consistent with that which is said about the One who saves, as they are one and the same God.[117] In addition, and foundational to this particular theological excursion, is the biblical witness that the One who creates deems that creation to be "very good" (Genesis 1:31).[118] Specifically, this excursion rejects the Hellenistic attitude that the material world is doomed, corrupt, and must be escaped; looking at a damned creation for clues as to the nature of God will only lead us further down the path of destruction, domination, and death that humanity has already long trod. Thus, the "theology from below" of this essay is grounded in the awesomeness of creation, the beauty and majesty of the created order that has been the subject of rhapsodic praise and song in the Jewish community from its formation.

Clues from Creation

In using a theology from below to discern the nature of God, the first thing we need to do is get over all squeamishness about sexual activity. Without making any correlative assertions germane to contemporary discussions about sexual orientation, Scripture clearly asserts that humans were created male and female, i.e., sexual beings, and we must assume that God found this aspect about us to be "very good," along with everything else that was made. There is simply no room for prudery in the glory of creation. Prudery is a mindset that comes as a consequence of humans poorly exercising free will. Thus, we can look basic sexual intimacy to get a glimpse at that which the Creator both made and found to be good.

Fathering

Many of the objections about the use of the word "Father" for God revolve around observations about how human males have behaved as fathers. However, the intrinsic aspects of the created order do not dictate the manner in which a human might choose to act *after* he has become a father. The birth of a child is not the beginning of the process of becoming a father, but the final stage. Moreover, humans, in behaving as fathers, have few if any characteristics that can be applied uniformly to all of them, especially throughout history. There are perhaps many things which culture and society say a father *ought* to be or do, but in reality no one can be or do all of the things which all cultures and societies in all times have declared to be part of fatherhood. Finally, certainly in contemporary Western culture, it can be observed that, for better or worse, there is precious little that fathers do which mothers do not also do. (The obverse is also true.) The varieties of expressions of father*hood* indicate that the role that a given father plays, or the behavior a particular father exhibits, is not part of the inherent created order. If we were to assert that Jesus addressed God as "Abba" because of some uniquely "fatherly" aspect of behavior exhibited by God towards "his" child, we would be hard-pressed to find in the scriptures an observable or experiential justification for the statement. When Jesus describes God as Father, he does not say what God did to be called that. We must explore further to find something that all fathers have in common and which may also be said of God.

If focusing on father*hood* cannot tell us about the uniform experience of being a father, then we must go back to an earlier point in the process: that of father*ing*. In this we find utter commonality amongst all biological fathers: in the process of becoming a human parent, the biological father gives of himself to the mother. He does not do this merely psychologically, he does it physically. The man actually empties himself, giving part of his body, his *self*, to another person. In this observation lies the clue in creation in which we can discern God as Father. Before we do that, however, the role of a woman in becoming a mother needs to be explored.

Mothering

The same analysis that we used to discern the unique aspect of the male in becoming a biological father can be applied to a woman in becoming a biological mother. The behavioral roles mothers play are simply not uniform enough to be useful in coming up with a determination of what it means to *be* a mother. To go back to the common ground of all mothers in *becoming* mothers, it is that they received something given by another. Again, this gives us a clue about how we can think about God, because this observation about mothering is a fact about God's creation.

The Holy Trinity

The Essentials of the Trinity

In looking at creation for clues about God, a recurring theme throughout the cosmos is the interdependence of elements and activities within a system or process. For a process to begin, there must be a concurrence of elements in time prior to a given outcome. For example, to have a fire, there must be, in the same place at the same time, fuel, oxygen, and a source of heat energy. If any one of those elements is missing in place or in time, a fire cannot occur. But for the presence of the fuel, the fire cannot occur; the same can be said of the oxygen and the heat source. Similarly, to have an embryo, there must be an egg and a sperm in the same hospitable place at the same time, or no embryo can result. If it were not for the simultaneous presence of the egg, *and* the sperm, *and* the hospitable environment, the process of becoming an embryo simply cannot begin. In these examples, no one of the elements takes *precedence* over the other; take any one of them away, and the process cannot begin; take any of them out during the process, and it cannot be completed.

The corollary to this is that the result of the conjunctions of element, place, and time is a transformation of the elements. After a fire, the fuel, oxygen, and energy that created the fire are transformed forever. Likewise, when an egg is fertilized, there is no longer egg and sperm, but only embryo. The elements have been transformed into something completely new.

The Events of the Trinity

Keeping the foregoing lessons from creation in mind, coupled with the scriptural witness, I dare now to explore the nature of the Trinity. First, we must remember that we exist in time, and "time is Nature's way to keep everything from happening at once."[119] Although God is eternal, we are humans who live temporally. We therefore need to consider things sequentially, because we live sequentially. The reason for clarifying this is because the process of events described below is not really consecutive, because if any one of the factors is removed at any time, the whole thing falls apart. Nonetheless, it is the only way humans can describe and assimilate information.

1. The Spirit of love. To imagine God in becoming the Triune God, we first need to posit a particular set of prerequisites to that becoming. First, God must exist in a context or milieu of divine, selfless, or agape Love. This "hospitable environment" is what permits total self-giving, or *kenosis* (Diagram 1). Selfless love requires an act of giving: "love isn't love 'til it's given away," as Oscar Hammerstein said. That which permits or enables self-giving must be ever-present in the processes of the Trinity, or the system turns into something else (which will be considered in Part IV). Thus, the presence of the Spirit of love is an essential element of the process of the Trinity.

CONTEXT
The Spirit of Love

Diagram 1

2. The Spirit of love and the act of self-giving. Within the Spirit of love, the first step in the becoming of the Trinity is for God to give Godself totally, in a kenotic event. Why? This we learn from scripture: "Love your neighbor as your*self*" (Mark 12:31a). God, in Jesus, commands us to love our *self*. This love is not the egotistical self-absorption of narcissism; it is regarding oneself as having intrinsic value. The opposite of *loving* ourselves is loathing ourselves or accounting ourselves as worthless. It is not only possible, but essential, that God follow God's commandment and give by loving Godself. Only in the loving of self is it possible for God to love others. Without a *giving* of a valued *self*, love of others is not possible.

This is the clue from creation that tells us that God is Father: the common, essential aspect of father*ing* in creation is giving of one's very *self*. God does not give something superfluous or adjunct to God, but in the process of becoming, self-empties.[120] God, in love, offers God's self totally, in an outpouring of radical, complete, and risky giving. God has given of God's very self, as a *father* does. This clue from creation, however, does not lead to the conclusion that God is male. To give of self in a *biological* sense helps us understand what father*ing* is, but it does not imply that any particular anatomy is necessary in a *non-biological* context. In this sense, then, "Father" means "the One who gives self."

The aspects of self-giving in the Spirit of love which must be emphasized are that the giving is both *complete* and *gratis*. In the complete, radical kenotic event, God gives, but has no requirement that anything be given back in return. In this process of giving of self, God does not demand, as part of the system, that something be rendered back. If that were done, the transfer would be only partial and would not be *kenosis*, or evacuation, because something would be held back. To be *gratis*, to be *gift*, the self-giving must be done with no strings attached. Otherwise, it would be in essence a business transaction, a sale. The command is to *love*, not to ask for love. In total, uncompensated self-giving, God takes the first step to loving.

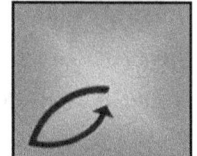

Giving is Fathering

Diagram 2

This *event* (as opposed to the "person") of the process of the Trinity is the second step in visualizing what is occurring (Diagram 2).

3. The Spirit of love and unconditional acceptance. In addition to prerequisites for giving, there is another essential element: to actually *give*, there must be something that *receives*. If someone sends something out and there is nothing to receive it, the item is merely mislaid, misplaced, or lost; it is not given.

Within the Spirit of love, there is *unconditional* acceptance. The One who Receives is one who takes in, enfolds, and embraces all of that which is given. This is not an infusion or imposition by a giver to a passive receptacle, but an active and joyous welcoming of that which is given. In the Spirit of love, the reception is done *gratis*, with no expectation of any benefit from either that which is given, or as a result of the acceptance. This is the clue from creation that tells us of the mothe*ring* nature of God: the complete and ecstatic acceptance of that which is offered. Again, conditions placed upon the receipt of any part of the offered gift changes the nature of the exchange from a free-will offering into a business deal. The second *event* of receiving is the third step in visualizing this concept (Diagram 3).

Receiving is Mothering

Diagram 3

4. The Spirit of love and transformation by loving in the Beloved Child. In receiving the gift, the receiver is perforce *changed*. The result of receiving the gift in the Spirit of love is that the receiver is reborn, transformed, made into a new creation. This is grounded in the Gospel of John, where Jesus says that one must be born from above, in the water and the spirit (John 3:3-5). The receiver's *self* is changed.

As this transformation of the receiver is the result of in an act of *self*-giving, i.e., *fathering*, the resulting new creation is the *child* of the One who gives. Inasmuch as this giving was done in the Spirit of love, the child is *beloved*. And, because there is now a child, the giver now has the title of Father. Note, however, that the giver is not yet a *beloved* father, inasmuch as the giver has not yet received love.

The Beloved Child is the same as the One who receives, and thus the receiver is not the child's "mother." The mothering, the receiving, is not something that results in a third entity, but transforms something that was already there. The receiving changes the *self* of the receiver by accepting the gift, and an act of love has now occurred (Diagram 4).

Transforming into the Beloved Child

Diagram 4

This giving and receiving now may legitimately described as God loving self.

5. Beloved Child gives in the Spirit of love. The Beloved Child of the Father is in the same "hospitable environment" as the Father: within the Spirit of love. By giving within the Spirit of love, the Beloved Child engages in the same kenotic, *gratis* self-giving as the Father did in the first event.[121] This giving of love is an act of *fathering*. The community of the Trinity is becoming apparent: the child is complying with the second commandment to love one's neighbor (Diagram 5). The cycle is not yet complete, however, because the love given by the child has yet to be received by anyone. A gift is not complete until it is received.

Beloved Child Gives in the Spirit of Love

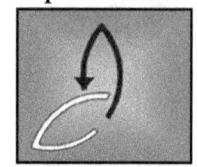

Diagram 5

6. In the Spirit of love, the giver receives. The completion of the first cycle of love is dependent on the first giver, *i.e.* the Father, unconditionally accepting the gift of the Beloved Child's self in the Spirit of love. This gives a new dimension to the Father in that the Father is also now a receiver, and is therefore mothering (Diagram 6).

The Father, in receiving, is Mothering

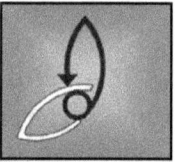

Diagram 6

7. Transformation by loving. The original Father, in unconditionally accepting and receiving the gift of the original Beloved Child's self in the Spirit of love, is *transformed* into a new creation. The giver is not now just Father, but Beloved Father: "Abba" (Diagram 7).

The Receiver Transforms into a New Creation: Beloved Father

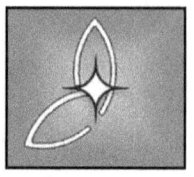

Diagram 7

8. Beloved Father gives in the Spirit of love. The work of the Spirit continues, as the Beloved Father continuous the kenotic outpouring of self in the Spirit of love. Now the Father is not only loving self, but is loving another, a neighbor (Diagram 8).

Beloved Father Gives in the Spirit of Love

Diagram 8

9. Beloved Child receives from the Beloved Father. This gift of self from the Beloved Father is received by the Beloved Child. In this receiving, the child accepts all of the realities of the Beloved Father. What happens to and within the one happens to and within the other. [Diagram 9]

Beloved Child Receives

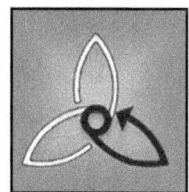

Diagram 9

10. Transformation by loving. In the unconditional, embracing, and enfolding love by which the Beloved Child receives the love of the Beloved Father, the Beloved Child is again transformed into a new creation: the Triune God (Diagram 10).

TRIUNE GOD

Diagram 10

The cycle is now both complete and eternal, as the events of giving, receiving, and transforming in the Spirit of love continue as the generative, creative, loving reality that is the form and source of all that was, and is, and shall be.

The Triune God is eternally giving, receiving, and transforming within the "Immanent Trinity." All of creation "lives and moves and has its being" within this constant, continuing divine conversation (see, generally, Moltmann). This has enormous implications for the nature and purpose of creation.

Creation by the Triune God

The approach to the Triune God outlined above results in the participants in the Trinity engaging in a "great conversation" wherein "creation happens in that the Father, Son, and Spirit mention among themselves others than themselves, so that they must be."[122] It is this Triune God who can now create by and with and in love, making the creation, nay, *singing* the creation in an ecstasy of loving:

> In thinking about "creation through the word," we should not therefore think primarily in metaphors of command and obedience. A better image is *the song of creation*. The word names, differentiates and appraises. But the breath is the same in all the words, and binds the words together.

> So the Creator differentiates his creatures through his creative Word and joins them through his Spirit, who is the sustainer of all his words. In the quickening breath and through the form-giving word, the Creator sings out his creatures in the sounds and rhythms in which he has his joy and his good pleasure. That is why there is something like *a cosmic liturgy* and *music of the spheres*.[123]

This brings us back to one of our first precepts: Creation is *good*, and we are part of it, a result of the joy and pleasure of the Triune God.

There is only one point in history when the eternal cycle was in any manner disrupted: during the life of the historical Jesus. It is at that point that the Beloved Child became specifically a *Son*, because it is not until that point that a biological differentiation was needed. This adjustment in the cycle also made possible the atoning actions of the Triune God. Jesus, the Son, loved his Father by doing that which his neighbor, his Father, needed to be reconciled with humanity; he experienced humanity's deepest pain: despair over the very presence of God, and yet at the same time died with the message of forgiveness on his lips.[124] Likewise, with the death of the Beloved Son, the Father suffered the agony of being separated from the child, and the Spirit of Love suffered the disruption of the unity and conversation between the Father and Child.[125] Nonetheless, the extraordinary, reconciling, and creating power of God's love began immediately to heal the rupture, to set things right, by overcoming death. Not only did this restore the Triune conversation, but the risen Christ returned to his terrified disciples, not to chastise and punish, but to forgive and renew his trust in their relationships. In relying on the power of love, God rejected the validity of power based on force or control of another:

> Nowhere is the truth of our sin more exposed to the light of God's judgment [than at the cross]. God rejects it and judges it precisely by refusing to have anything to do with it. God will have nothing to do with our violence, our claim to be free, our drives to dominate. There is nothing God can or will do but die at our hands: bear our sins. . . .

[Jesus] is not a hero for our systems. He is not vindicated by us. He is vindicated by God.[126]

In the power of love, God raised Jesus and overcame the power of death. The Beloved Son "ascended," restored to the original "place" and the eternal cycle was resumed, enriched, and transformed by the temporal, historical life and death of the Beloved Child. What happened to Jesus forever became an event in the life of God.

The above approach attempts to explain why Jesus addressed God as Father: God gave of Godself, in transforming love, and the Beloved Child was begotten. Jesus did not pray to God as Mother, even though the maternal is inherent in God (Luke 13:34). God as Mother accepts our attempts to love, in our brokenness, our suffering, and is transformed by our love. What *we*, in the Spirit, do toward God is how God can even be a mother to us. But what God does for us is how God is a father to us. The instant we are in a dynamic where the flow of love is going from God towards us, we are relating to God as Father, the Father whose sends the Spirit, who sends love. In that case, *we* are the receiver, the mother, who is transformed by God. The full and humble willingness to receive God's unconditional love, even at personal cost, is the grace and example given by Mary, the mother of Jesus.

The next task is to briefly explore two issues: the consequences of the absence of the Spirit of love in any of the events of the Trinity, and the ramifications of our temporal existence on and within the life of the Triune God.

Unholy Trinity

An "unholy" Trinity results when any of the giving or receiving described above is done without the sanctifying presence of the Spirit of love. Briefly:

The initial "giving" is done with the expectation of some return.

If the initial giving is done with the expectation of some benefit or return from the recipient, then the transaction is not a *gift*. It is either a sale (if the giver expects some sort of payment) or a bailment (if the giver expects the receiver to simply preserve that which was given).

If the transaction is a sale, the recipient is transformed into a *debtor* until payment is made. A hierarchical relationship is formed, because the giver is a creditor and has rights against the debtor. Thus, within the Immanent Trinity, the relationship of the "father" and "child" are ones of duty and tribute, of power and control.

Applying this to creation, a creditor-debtor situation arises if the creating love of God is viewed as something other than a free gift. If God's divine love is something that we, as nondivine humans, simply cannot return in full, then a debtor/creditor relationship is created. In this situation, "reconciliation" with God, i.e., forgiveness of the debt, requires the penal subsitutionary atonement theory of the "Latin" or "objective" type.[127]

Alternatively, the transaction might be a bailment, similar to when we give our car to a valet parking attendant. In a bailment, the recipient is transformed into a bailee or *custodian*. The custodian has no right to change the thing given; the giver remains in control. Within the Trinity, this creates a divine Son who does the will of the Father in heaven because he has no choice, no freedom to change the law, wisdom, or plans of the Father. In such a relationship, Jesus would not have been free to refuse the cup in Gethsemane.

With regard to humanity, the creation of a custodial relationship between God and humanity would mean that people were entrusted with God's life, expectations, and commandments, bound by legal constraints, and regarded by a dispassionate divine wisdom. Such a God is immutable, unresponsive: God does not so much give as impose, and we take. It is this type of God that feminist theologians understandably reject.[128] The method for atonement in this construct is at least compliant obedience, and at best disciplined excellence in religious achievement, so that our *behavior* be as much as possible like Jesus's.[129]

The initial receiving is conditioned on the acceptability of the gift.

Another way to corrupt the Trinity and make it unholy is if the receiver accepts the gift conditionally. If the recipient does not unconditionally accept in love that which the giver offers, then part of the gift—and the giver—is rejected. The recipient is not transformed, only gratified. This is like shopping in a grocery store: the store is full of items, but the only goods selected are those that the purchaser desires. The rest is left alone.

In the Immanent Trinity, if the proffered love is taken only insofar as it meets the needs of the recipient, the love becomes food. The giver gives, and the receiver consumes. This relationship is a one-way street, and the loving giver will never be able to satisfy and transform the receiver. This is the type of consuming "love" displayed by the demon Wormwood throughout C.S. Lewis' *The Screwtape Letters*.[130]

Within creation, if humanity takes only part of God's gifts, then we too are merely consumers of creation. We take only that part of creation that suits our priorities, and do not accept the rest of the aspects of God's loving gift: the wholeness and beauty of creation, which is interdependent and communal. Not only do we refuse part of the gift, we have no hesitation to use our powers of control and violence when we do not receive what we *do* want fast enough. In this manner we oppress creation, while carefully avoiding considering how long we can go on receiving and consuming only a portion of God's loving gift. If we do not unconditionally accept the entirety of the gift of God's love, and the resulting transformation into new creatures, born from above, we will continue to corrupt and poison ourselves, others, and the earth on which we all live.

In sum, the events of the unholy trinity, where actions are not taken in love but in shortsighted self-interest, are events leading to death and violence.

Being Perfect

Jesus calls us to emulate the self-giving love of the Holy Trinity: "For if you love those who love you, what reward do you have? . . . Be perfect, therefore, as your heavenly Father is perfect" (Matthew 5:46a, 48). We are also called to be unconditionally accepting of the Love of God, and thus transformed by being born from above (John 3:3-5). We can hope to be in the community of the Triune God because the dynamics of the Immanent Trinity include creation, and we are creatures made in the image and likeness of God.

Because God's essence and work are not twofold but one, it would follow that God's relationship to the world is one of becoming one with the world, healing it to become perfect. This becoming one with the world accomplishes our salvation by taking up human life into the perfect, utterly holy event of God's being.[131]

In looking at the dynamics of the Immanent Trinity, and the yearning of the Triune God to be in identical relationship with humanity, we can begin to understand what it means to "be perfect."

First, acting as a father has nothing to do with domination, oppression, or primacy.[132] To *father* as God fathers means to give oneself totally. This aspect of fathering is certainly not dependent on biology: Everybody, regardless of anatomy, is called to this way of being perfect. Just as God's name is not to be confused with God's functions,[133] neither is our identity in the community to be limited by our biological functions.

Similarly, the process of perfecting or healing creation is God's work.[134] The creator of heaven and earth is already reconciling the powers that will, in the end, save God's beloved creation and restore it to the perfection for which it was originally meant.

For Christians, being perfect means doing what God asks of us, which begins by listening to God's prayer, already being prayed in us.[135] Through the process of perfection, Christians learn what it means to accept the Spirit of love unconditionally, and be born from above — be made into a new creation.

In being so transformed into the adopted, beloved children of God, we enter into the cycle of giving, receiving, and transformation of the Triune God. That means we relate not only to God within this cycle, but we reach out to others in precisely the same manner as God reaches out to us. Within the Spirit of love, we are called to give and receive, to transform and be transformed, here with our brothers and sisters and mothers in creation (Mark 3:35).

Misdirected Trust or Misfiring Neurons
Theology and Science and a Study of Sin

Anna Madsen

"Just shut up and believe!'

Walt loved telling the story of the time when he screwed up his courage in confirmation to say to his pastor, notably also his father, that he still didn't understand the Holy Spirit.

That was the answer he got: "Just shut up and believe!"

Every time he told this tale, Walt's head went down, his hands went up, and though he didn't laugh out loud, you could hear his voice rise in barely contained glee.

Imagine my own glee when, researching for this very *Gedenkschrift* in honor of Walt, I stumbled on this sentence, "You can do perfectly good physics if you just 'shut up and calculate!'"[136] We have Max Tegmark to thank for the scientific version of Walt's father's command. Tegmark is a physicist at MIT who believes that all of life is simply expressed mathematics and can be understood by simply applying mathematical postures and formulae.

Now Walt was never one to wither in the face of a contrary position: he was famous for saying that there are all sorts of reasons in the world; it was just that some reasons are better than others.

Let's be clear: he thought his reasons were awfully good.

At the same time, he would not simply say, "Shut up and believe." Walt loved the intellectual chase of a new idea, of a debate that informed and challenged, of the dawning of a new insight, of the culling of knowledge from across disciplines. From him I learned that every part of a library can interest me; some parts do not interest me as much as others, true, but because God relates to all things, all things relate to God. Given that, it behooves us to learn about as many things as we can.

It is with deep respect, then, that I use this contribution to this volume as a way to consider and re-consider Walt's notion of sin. I've been asked to address the nature and mission of the church. It seems to me that forgiveness evidences a most radical mark of the risen Jesus, and itself can be stewarded as a sign of the reign of God. But, given new knowledge from the fields of neurology and psychology, Walt's definition of sin as "misdirected trust" might, left at that, no longer be sufficient either as a way to grasp what moves someone to sin or as a way to consider an appropriate response to those who engage in sin.

Walt, of course, took his cue for his understanding about sin from his working definition of God: God is that in which or in whom you place your ultimate trust. He's certainly standing firm in the Lutheran tradition with that description, one on which I continue to depend.

It is no great leap, then, to define sin as "misdirected trust." That is, we put our faith in that which is undeserving of it. As Walt liked to say, the penultimate can't bear the weight of our ultimacy.

Walt was certainly consistent in his theology, a theology that was overtly, unapologetically, and organically constructed on, grounded in, threaded through, and bracketed by the events of the Triduum. As he saw it, then, we are finite and free: we have finite freedom. Within the bounds of our birth and our death, and in our encounters with our God, we have the capacity to—and we do—make choices. A la Pannenberg, Walt believed that we are "open to the future," able to "transcend time and space through memory and imagination."

From this place, Walt made the case that sin was not an instance of immorality, or about morals; it was rather a case of seeking immortality, of keeping a feared or certain death at bay. Conversion, then, is the decision to no longer seek to save ourselves by self-justification, by denying the reality of death, or by preserving our lives at the expense of others. Conversely, he taught, conversion frees us to throw ourselves in trust into the reign of God, and into the service of Jesus.

The train of thought here is inherently, internally, consistently flowing from the definition of God as that in which one ultimately trusts. Trust in Easter, and you are free. Trust in death, trust in fear, trust in self, trust in self-preservation, and you are bound and are misdirecting your trust.

The trouble is, I have come to wonder whether it is that simple.

Both the working definition of God and the working definition of sin assume some basic ability to make a choice to trust—misdirected or otherwise—to be free to discern, to have the transcendent ability to opt for the reign of God and opt out of a way of life that is dooming and ultimately doomed.[137] My concerns about this approach are manifold. Perhaps my most powerful objections, however, regard the way in which this take on sin isolates the sinner, removes any responsibility for the crisis from the larger community, and lays the groundwork for the sinner's shame and guilt. If, that is, one can trust in God, but opts instead to trust in something not-God, then one has made a bad choice.

Ironically, I think that the potential effect of Walt's thinking on sin accomplishes one of the last things that he would wish: a lack of compassion for those who have engaged in sinful behavior and a reduction of the complex reasons for their actions to a simple matter of choice. But these closing words about sin found in his May 6 lecture, left as they are anyway, run the risk of leading us to that very tendency: "The Christian statement about humanity . . . begins with the recognition that what is unique about our humanity is our capacity for self-transcendence in the midst of our finitude. We are capable of evaluating and being evaluated."

For some time, then, I have sat at the feet of experts in the field of biology and psychology and neurology, hoping to learn from them why people behave as they do. What is it, from their perspective, that drives someone to engage in behavior that is destructive to themselves and others, given this purported ability to self-evaluate?

Turns out, it's complicated.

Evolutionary psychologists, scientists who look at behavior from a Darwinian tack, note that across cultures, people seem to be driven to achieve social standing and also experience guilt. Robert Wright, journalist, author, and scholar in the fields of the sciences, history, and religion, writes of humanity having "knobs" and "tuners," correlated to genes and environment. Certain elements of human existence are established according to genetic determinism, but these "knobs" are adjusted according to the environment in which we each sit.[138] For example, Wright maintains that contemporary Darwinism recognizes that the community in which people live propels the inhabitants of that context to behave in a certain way. Studies to which he points demonstrate that moral behavior in smaller, more static communities tend toward communal cooperative strategies, cultural mechanisms that propel people toward "reciprocal altruism," a cyclical habit of benefiting those who benefit you and the community via a premium placed on integrity and honesty.

Why these two values? Small locales (towns, even neighborhoods and places of business) illustrate one reason. If you are a known quantity and are understood to be a person of either good or ill repute, your stock and stake in the community rise or fall accordingly. Conversely, in places where there is rampant poverty and transience—let alone lower life expectancies—the stakes to maintain one's reputation are lower, the need to facilitate communal well-being less pressing, and the compulsion to protect one's own interests more urgent.[139] As Wright says, "To some it will sound odd to hear Darwinians describing criminals as 'victims of society' rather than as victims of faulty genes. But that's one difference between Darwinism at the turn of this century and at the turn of the last. Once you think of genes as programming behavioral development, and not just behavior, as molding the young mind to fit its context—then we all start to look like victims (or beneficiaries) of our environment, no less than of our genes."[140] In this excerpt, hear the word "victim" not as a euphemism for moral exoneration. Instead, Wright attempts to help us see that even the notion of moral "choice" is not objectively obvious or true, but is rather determined by knobs (genes) and tunings (environment).[141]

Not everyone, however, agrees with the determinism evidenced by Wright. Scientist, doctor, and author Jeffrey M. Schwartz specializes in the treatment of Obsessive Compulsive Disorder (OCD) patients, and his work with this disorder propelled him into research beyond OCD, and rather toward the possibility of validating the role of the mind and of free will—something that materialists like Wright stridently mock.

Wasting no time to make his case, Schwartz asserts,

> For if we truly believe, when the day is done, that our mind and all that term entails—the choices we make, the reactions we have, the emotions we feel are nothing but the expression of a machine governed by the rules of classical physics and chemistry, and that our behavior follows ineluctably from the workings of our neurons, then we're forced to conclude that the subjective sense of freedom is a "user illusion." Our sense that we are free to make moral decisions is a cruel joke, and society's insistence that individuals (with exceptions for the very young and mentally ill) be held responsible for their actions is no more firmly rooted in reason than a sand castle is rooted in the beach. In stark contrast to the current paradigm, however, the merging research on neuroplasticity, attention, and the causal efficacy of will supports the opposite view—one that demands the recognition of moral responsibility.[142]

In other words, Schwartz believes that we have a choice to trust in one thing or another, despite centuries of scientific dogma that states the contrary. We are more than automatons of our genes and environment.

Schwartz points to Descartes as the key modern architect of our deterministic view of human behavior. To come to some sense of that which composes the "mental realm," Descartes divvied up reality into two segments: *res cogitans*, the arena of thought, and *res extensa*, namely, the realm of the material. Given that the mind is something that cannot be quantified or tested because it has no "heft," Descartes relegated it to the concern not of science, but of the church.[143] And both disciplines were fine with that. Science abdicated interest in the mind, theology abdicated interest in the brain. In the process, however, both arenas suffered the effects of a knowledge lobotomy, to so speak, each losing the benefit of shared insight flowing in both directions.

In *The Mind and the Brain*, Schwartz reviews how the mind as an object of study and a facet of reality became a taboo notion in the scientific community, and even mockable. Modern science views "[a]nything nonphysical . . . at best an artifact, at worst an illusion."[144] There was some nod to its existence by those who acknowledged non-physical mental actions (thoughts, choices, ideas, and so forth), but these events were then attributed them to quantifiable and predictable synaptic activity. "Mind, the theory goes, is just brain with more lyrical allusions. Neural correlates to every aspect of mind you can think of are not merely correlates; they are the essence of that aspect of mind," says Schwartz.[145] The activities of the mind are just expressed brain activity.

But Schwartz makes the case that the mind does, as such, exist and engages in regular interplay with the brain. Vis-à-vis the topic for this essay, contrary to the determinism of modern day science, Schwartz champions the real existence of volition, of free will, thereby allowing us to make choices. "For if we truly believe, when the day is done, that our mind and all that term entails—the choices we make, the reactions we have, the emotions we feel—are nothing but the expression of a machine governed by the rules of classical physics and chemistry, and that our behavior follows ineluctably from the workings of our neurons, then we're forced to conclude that the subjective sense of freedom is a 'user illusion,'" he says.[146]

That is, if the world is indeed only "material," how does a thought exist? Volition? Consciousness? Transcendence?

And why should we have any investment then in the course of our lives, individual and shared? Was Macbeth not right, that we are only poor players on a stage, and the producer of our actions is the all-powerful brain to whom we must innately pay obeisance?

Schwartz's work with patients who suffer from OCD has lead him to upend this prevailing view of the mind/brain relationship, and uncover astonishing discoveries about the brain's plasticity and the mind's ability to shape, by way of thought, the actual physical structure of the brain. His revelations suggest that by repeated intentional focus and attention on certain behaviors, the brain's skids, so to speak, will become greased in such a way that the new neurocircuitries will be grown where they were lacking, and previously established negative neurocircuitries will begin to wither and wane.

OCD is a perfect disease to use as a case study, for OCD sufferers are plagued with persistent and utterly unwelcome recurring impulses to engage behaviors that the patient actually knows are unwanted, unnecessary, and ultimately harmful. A unique marker to OCD is that these ritualistic impulses are "ego-dystonic," which is to say that they and the correlating actions are utterly inconsistent with the person's own self-awareness and desires. In other words, someone who feels compelled to ritualistically wash hands is fully aware that it is unwarranted and destructive on any number of levels; still, they cannot quash the impulse.[147]

Schwartz's studies demonstrate that a four-step process can severely check the compulsions. He re-labels urges as symptoms of a brain's "false signals instead of indications that they are 'crazy'," reattributing their fixations to misfires within their brain's circuitry rather than a real need to succumb to the feeling, refocusing their impulse onto another activity, and revaluing their OCD tendencies so that rather than having consummate power, the urges have only the power that the individual chooses to give to them. With this four-fold approach, success for his patients has been wildly powerful, and wildly popular.

Not only can Schwartz anecdotally demonstrate the positive outcomes of his approach. Functional MRIs taken before and after therapy show how areas of the brain triggered by OCD compulsivity were significantly active prior to the initiation of the treatment. However, as the treatment progressed and came to an end, these focal points were lessened. New areas were instead activated, ones that circumvented the negative behavioral neural connections. The non-physical thoughts had a demonstrable physical effect on the brain, a remarkable discovery: a non-physical force changed the brain physically.

Schwartz's revolutionary approach came not only from hunches, from experience with his patients, and from studying MRIs, but also from observations about quantum physics and collaboration with experts in the field. He and his physicist colleague Henry Stapp uncovered corollaries between quantum behaviors and human behaviors at the level of the mind's volition. The implications are tantalizing.

Quantum physics asserts the bizarre and utterly counter-intuitive claim that something does not exist unless it is observed. Simply by posing a question, by seeking to quantify something, a phenomenon is called into reality. This essential claim of quantum physics distressed Albert Einstein, and yet has been repeatedly demonstrated to be true. "In classical physics, observed systems have an existence independent of the mind that observes and probes them. In quantum physics, however, only through an act of observation does a physical quantity come to have an actual value," says Schwarz.[148] This experience is called the "collapse of the wave function," and named or not, no one quite understands it. They, do, however, agree that it is a real phenomenon: the simple act of observing something restricts its options from being many to being the single one observed. "Matter," Schwartz says later, "has become intrinsically connected to subjective experiences."[149]

The implications for the power of the will to effect behavioral changes are great. Intentionally focusing on a desired change in behavior yields not only a change in the behavior, but a change in the brain, which is precisely that which effects the change in the behavior. As I've argued elsewhere,[150] psychologists and neurologists have much to offer us by way of increasing empathy and compassion on those who sin, regardless of whether we sin on small or on a grand scale. Horrific abuse and boundless love, brain injuries and omega-3s, exhaustion and physical fitness, serotonin and anti-depressants contribute to overall brain health and, therefore, behavior.

After reading Schwartz's book, however, I realized that I had fallen into a deterministic trap, one about which I had some creeping awareness. Walt's notion of sin propelled me to investigate whether or not sin is as simple as a choice. As a therapist once said to me, if a person is parched but no sweet, fresh water can be found, they will drink the tainted stuff. The need to quench a thirst is not a decision; it is primal. I am not "trusting" in my thirst; I am compelled to satiate it or die. It is, in keeping with Walt's words, a matter of mortality, not morality.

And yet invoking the language of "trust" implicitly suggests a measure of intentionality, for the very definition of "trust" ascribes "firm belief" to the action of trusting. But when brain chemistry is imbalanced, when PTSD is in play, when glucose levels are off, when abuse has grown the amygdala beyond its healthy proportions while shrinking the reasoning hippocampus, individuals don't choose to trust in anything: they are victims of both experience, genes, context, and traumas. They need redemption, not from sin but from their lot. "Transcending" time and space through memory and imagination is a luxury afforded to those who are not so afflicted.

My hope in presenting this information in recent years was not least of all compassion. People who sabotage themselves and others are motivated by desperation, and they are essentially helpless in the face of their circumstances. Who among us has not engaged in "sinful" behavior, and who among us can say that at that moment we were in a Sweet Spot of Life? Was it not consistently true that when we sinned we were in some way dysregulated, unhealthy, or traumatized? Is not the very context for our behavior itself in need of redemption?

While I stand by many of these assertions, it became very difficult for me to ascribe any sort of personal responsibility for vile, violent, and simply "sloppy" behavior. I could chalk up anyone's conduct to a chemical imbalance, an unstable childhood, or brain malformations caused by any number of reasons.

Ironically, as I was having trouble making anyone responsible for their behaviors because their actions were determined by mediating factors, I was also objecting to the ubiquitous idea of "God's Plan." I could not—and still cannot—bear the notion of God's Plan, for we then abdicate any responsibility, investment, or ownership in the goings-on of our lives. We are mere pawns of God, helpless in the face of God's deterministic power. But then, reading Schwartz, I realized that I had done the same thing by way of moral/mortal behavior: I had been espousing that we are mere pawns of our genes and environment, and are helpless in the face of their deterministic power.

Schwartz has almost corrected my unmitigated absolution of any responsibility for behavior. He demonstrates that we can change our brains, that we can make changes, and that we can alter our behaviors.

What is logically possible, however, might not be actually possible. Even Schwartz acknowledges this truth when he writes about the capacity for the mind to express volition:

> There is danger to this way of thinking: it treads close to the position that anyone with a mental illness remains sick because of a failure of will, anyone with an undesirable personality train retains it because she has failed to exert sufficient mental effort. Even those of us who distrust the 'My genes (or my neurochemicals) made me do it' school of human behavior back away from the implication that will alone can bring into being the neural circuitry capable of supporting any temperament or behavioral tendency—indeed, any state of mental health. But to frame the issue in this all-or-nothing way is to create a simplistic, and false, choice.[151]

And here, finally, we get to the piece that might be manifestly missing from Walt's theology, but is utterly consistent with it: community. In a sentence that is but a nod and a wave to perhaps the critical piece in establishing the greatest potential of mental health—and the propensity to not engage in misdirected trust—Schwartz says, "...[a]lthough directed mental force allows will to change the brain in both the stroke patients Edward Taub has treated and my own OCD patients, of course it is not will alone. It is knowledge, training, support from the community and loved ones, and appropriate medical input."[152]

I wonder, as I further my studies on brain research, quantum physics, and sin, whether this notion of an external observing a reality, thereby creating a reality, might be a helpful assist to Walt's formulation about sin. People who sin are desperate to hang on, consciously or not, to some form of immortality: they are indeed trying to keep death at bay. Of this Walt was brilliantly right.

But individuals who sin (and larger groups, like nations, as Cynthia Moe-Lobeda illustrated with tremendous insight in her book, *Healing a Broken World: Globalization and God*[153]) are in any number of ways, and for any number of reasons, isolated. Their own myopia, shame, alienation from self or others, illness, prevents them from seeking comment and counsel from other points of view. Unobserved, their reality remains unchecked. Observed, their patterns, their behaviors, their sins are no longer free to roam and have wild freedom to reign, but are pinpointed, named, quantified, analyzed, and, perhaps, healed.

Schwartz's by-the-way comment about community may well hold the key for how salvation, how *soteria*, how health, healing, and wholeness can be restored in someone who is clinging to a false immortality, who is misdirecting their trust.

As for the church, then, it seems to me that we can be holy observers. We can be those who do not observe to judge, but to heal in community. Certainly, in Walt's teachings on baptism, there are elements here from which we can draw. In his lecture notes from May 15, 1996, he said, "Sin means not trusting Jesus as Messiah, not trusting the advent of the coming Kingdom." As I've attempted to illustrate above, it's not that simple, nor is an extrapolation he makes from that assertion: "On the one hand, sin takes the form of refusal to be sinners, that is, the destructive insistence on [sic] our own righteousness." Again, neurologists, biologists, and psychologists would be quite resistant, and with good reason, to distill all behavior which the church has and does call sinful to "the destructive insistence on our own righteousness."

However, Walt continues, "On the other hand, sin also takes the opposite form of the inability to recognize one's authentic significance as a creation and a person of God." His lecture flows from here into an exposition about communal confession and forgiveness. He found this liturgical ritual essential to the well-being of the church and the Christian community.

So do I.

But given what we can learn from scientists about the complexity of human behavior, I imagine that were he to rewrite his lecture today, he would see that sin is not simply about not trusting Jesus. And he would see that confession does not address the pain caused by the cascading troubles of someone in the grip of an illness like OCD.

Instead, I believe that Walt would use the sentence about our authentic significance as people of God to also emphasize that communal involvement as the Christian church shall be grounded in worship, but must also find regular, active, participatory, compassionate, hospitable, reconciling, forgiving, healing manifestations by way of medicinal assistance, of practical help, of active presence, of courageous interventions, of tireless support.

Over more than one martini or manhattan on more than one occasion, I have wished for Walt to still be here, to be sitting across from me in my living room, to listen to my pushback, to correct and clarify, and maybe, just maybe, to sigh and say, "Perhaps you have a point."

Depending on the day and how much I miss him, I'd even be grateful for a "Just shut up and believe!"

Walter Bouman taught me many things: to shut up, not so much. But Walt's wisdom and profundity and humility taught me not only knowledge, not only his "system," not only how justification translates into justice, not only to delight in God's *tov meod* creation, but to believe more strongly in and act more freely out of the promise of the resurrection of Jesus the Christ. Walt did that.

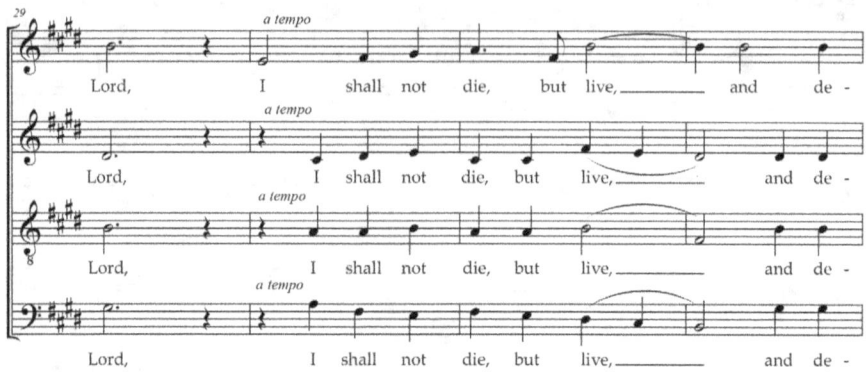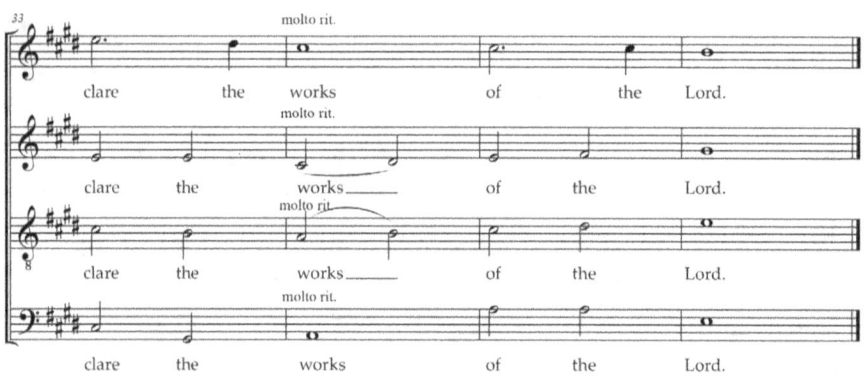

Dying and Living

Nancy Raabe

> But not for that dream I on this strange course,
> But on this travail look for greater birth. . . .
> Come, lady, die to live.
>
> William Shakespeare, *Much Ado About Nothing*,
> Act 4, Scene 1

In this passage from *Much Ado About Nothing*, Shakespeare's Friar Francis is concocting a plan to rescue Hero after a monumental case of mistaken identity. She is to undergo a temporary death, he urges her father Leonato to accept, so as to allow for a permanent life together with Claudio.

In this context, "die to live" heralds a worldly sequence of events. But Christians will recognize in these three words the affirmation that God, in God's grace and mercy, rescues us from death by bringing us to new life. To Bouman, this new life means "the end of the 'law' (that is, our way of justifying ourselves, or our basis for hating ourselves), the end of the power of death (that is, our quest for self-protection at the expense of others), the end of sin (that is, our refusal to trust God, to trust the Gospel)" and "the end of the powers of the 'old age.' . . . We cannot now be alienated from God and God's love. The new age has come, and it is the age of the Holy Spirit."[154]

In selecting a text for his musical work to honor Walt Bouman, Carl Schalk was drawn to Psalm 118:17:

> There are glad songs of victory in the tents of the righteous:
> "The right hand of the Lord does valiantly;
> the right hand of the Lord is exalted;
> the right hand of the Lord does valiantly."
> I shall not die, but live, and declare the works of the Lord.
> (Psalm 118:14-17)

This was an inspired decision—not only for its articulation of the conviction that resides at the heart of the Christian faith, expressed by Paul in Romans 6:8-11,[155] but also for the way in which the text pays tribute to Bouman's deep admiration for Martin Luther.

Carl Schalk, Composer and Proclaimer of the Gospel

For this volume, composer Carl Schalk was asked to contribute an article that recognized Bouman's passion for and deep understanding of the music of the church.

Schalk and Bouman were well acquainted from their days together on the faculty of Concordia Teachers College. Schalk likes to tell the story of how he first met Bouman early in his time there. Bouman was holding forth before a group on a theological topic. Perhaps unaware that few dared question Bouman's positions, Schalk raised his hand at one point and said in his simple, direct way, "No, I don't think so." While Bouman was initially startled that someone would openly disagree with him, he and Schalk quickly became good friends.[156]

In place of an essay, Schalk decided instead to add to the great body of church music. The product is his new motet "I Shall Not Die, But Live" on Psalm 118:17, reproduced in this volume on pages [156-160] and dedicated to Bouman.

Now in his mid-80s, Schalk remains the vigorous advocate that he has always been for music as a primary element of worship. "The song of the church," Schalk emphasizes, "is a response of faith to what God has done in Jesus Christ. It is a song from the heart of the church to the heart of God, from the heart of the church to the heart of each believer, and from the heart of the church to the world."[157]

But more than that, Schalk never tires of emphasizing that the purpose of this song is to proclaim the gospel. This, he says, is the good news of salvation through Jesus Christ: God in the person of Jesus Christ was sent to us, he died and was buried, and on the third day he rose again, conquering death forever.

Schalk considers it our duty and delight in our hymnody and liturgy to bear witness to the Christian narrative. We sing not about who God is, but how God has acted on our behalf; we sing of the hope that Christ brings for the future. "There we tell the story that makes us a Christian community," Schalk has said. "The formation of Christians young and old is carried out by the handing over of the words of faith as contained in the liturgy and hymnody. We *must* teach the faith of the church, and not our own ideas."[158]

Layers of Significance

There are layers of significance in Schalk's decision to honor Bouman by means of Psalm 118:17.

Read in the context of the gospel, the verse affirms the resurrection and our eternal lives in Christ. Bouman writes, "The future in Christ inaugurates already here and now the reign of God and its ultimate consummation when the powers of 'this age'—including sin and death, transiency and disappointment—are visibly disclosed to be subject to the Messiah (1 Corinthians 15:24-28). That is, they have no power because of Jesus the Christ. The inbreaking of the reign of God is a proleptic vision of the outcome of history in the midst of history."[159]

Second, the text exhorts us to proclaim all that God has done. In our new lives in Christ, we are to *"declare* the works of the Lord."

Third, by using it, Schalk honors Martin Luther, an accomplished musician in his own right,[160] from whose deep well of writings Bouman drew so often.[161] Schalk knew that Psalm 118:17 was one of Martin Luther's favorite passages in all scripture. Robin Leaver affirms that this verse "became in effect Luther's motto." [162]

Finally, Schalk's choice of text links Luther's deep convictions about music and theology with Bouman's own. Both understood well that, next to theology, there was no greater power than music with which to repel death and the devil. Bouman addressed this pointedly in his keynote speech for the Constituting Convention of the Association of Lutheran Church Musicians at St. Olaf College in August 1986 (reproduced in the Appendix of this volume), when he cited Luther's brief *Skizze peri tes mousikes*, penned during his confinement at Coburg Castle in 1530.[163]

Martin Luther's Motet *Non moriar sed vivam*

In yet another reason for the significance of Schalk's use of this verse, Luther used it (in its Latin form, *Non moriar, sed vivam, et narrabo opera Domine*) for what was to become his only polyphonic composition.[164]

Luther's deep affinity for the text emerged out of a momentous chain of events.

His six months in isolation at Coburg in 1530 during the Imperial Diet of Augsburg were dreary and pocked with despair. The Duke of Saxony had forbidden him to attend the Diet out of fear that Luther might be nabbed and burned as a heretic. Although he tried to remain abreast of events there, Luther became increasingly despondent as the long days dragged on. The antiphon he had long cherished on Psalm 4:8 — "I will both lie down and sleep in peace; for you alone, O Lord, make me lie down in safety" — haunted him constantly.

The Diet had opened with the motet *Ecce quam bonum* by Luther's good friend Ludwig Senfl, a master who Luther greatly admired. Based on Psalm 133 ("How very good and pleasant it is when kindred live together in unity"), Senfl's motet was astutely gauged to the proceedings of the Diet, which in part concerned the effort to reconcile Lutheran and Roman Catholic theological positions.

Learning of Senfl's *Ecce quam bonum*, Luther sent a heartfelt letter to his friend begging him to compose a work on Psalm 4:8 for Luther's own consolation. "I hope that the end of my life is at hand," he wrote. "The world hates me and cannot bear me."[165]

Senfl not only honored this request but also but also sent a motet on Psalm 118:17; he knew Luther also treasured this text. Robin Leaver tells us that this verse "was a great comfort to the Wittenberg Reformer, isolated as he was in Coburg Castle away from the action in Augsburg."[166] In fact, Luther arranged for this verse and the accompanying chant to be carved into the wall of his castle room.[167] We may conjecture, then, that it was not only this but the comfort the music his esteemed friend had provided him during those dark months of isolation in 1530, that led Luther years later to return to Psalm 118:17 for a motet of his own, *Non moriar, sed vivam.*

From Luther to Schalk

Luther loved music and grasped its vast potential. "Of all the Protestant reformers of his time," Carl Schalk writes, "only Martin Luther unhesitatingly commended the use of music in the nourishment of the Christian life and in the worship of the church."[168]

We see Luther's understanding of the mechanics of music in this economical four-voice motet. While Senfl's setting[169] unfolds as a succession of single lines ascending and descending in points of imitation, Luther explores greater possibilities for tone painting. Around the *cantus firmus* in the tenor, the other voices are shimmering web of rising and falling lines, each bearing its own integrity of shape but moving in response to the motion of the others. The lively contrapuntal texture coalesces around two internal structural points, the cadences at the statement and repetition of *"sed vivam,"* but flows freely again and until they all are joined together in the smooth movement into the final cadence.

Taken at a tempo appropriate to the time in which the semibreve approximates the pace of an average person at rest (sixty to eighty beats per minute), Luther's *Non moriar* clocks in at less than thirty seconds.[170] But even in this brief span it bears witness to the extraordinary reach of the Reformer's intellect and the musical ability that brought him acclaim.

Luther's motet must have been sounding somewhere in Schalk's mind as he crafted his own approach to this text. In contrast to Senfl and Luther, we find Schalk more purposeful in his tone painting. His two-measure central motive captures perfectly the image of moving from death to life. The rising fourth outlined at the outset contains within it the promise of something beyond this mortal life, while the Christian conviction of hope is made palpable in the leap up to the scale's fifth degree (for example, the E up to the B in m. 2) that immediately follows. The turn from death to life is profiled by the brief turn downward (A to the eighth-note F-sharp in m. 2), and the joyful propulsion to the fifth degree of the scale that completes this opening gesture.

Harmonious parallel voices emphasize the conviction of hope contained in the rising lines that carry the first phrase of the verse ("I shall not die, but live"), which extends through the downbeat of m. 17. The second phrase of text is then launched abruptly by a proclamatory rising fourth that unfurls in points of imitation before the voices then join together in parallel rising and falling thirds and sixths. The climax of the setting occurs in m. 24-27 as the sopranos and altos mount up on "declare the works of the Lord," with the sopranos dramatically sustaining the last word, as the tenors and baritones follow in perfect imitation. The effect is to sustain this experiential high point for the duration of all four measures.

A coda, or denouement, follows starting in m. 30. It is made more reflective in character by the harmonization of the first note of the primary motive by the subdominant. In measure 32 all four voices finally come together, just as they did in the approach to the end of Luther's motet, for the final statement of "... and declare the works of the Lord." The downbeat of m. 33 is poignantly harmonized by the chord of the minor sixth. A plagal (IV-I) cadence, that familiar bow of reverence so common to the church, brings the motet to its conclusion.

"To die, to live": Carl Schalk and Jaroslav Vajda

Carl Schalk is represented generously throughout the sacred choral catalogue. Nonetheless he is best known for his hymn settings, which display fine craftsmanship and acute attention to the text and its theological implications. Many familiar with his entire body of music consider "Where Shepherds Lately Knelt," composed to a text by his longtime hymn-writing colleague Jaroslav Vajda, to be Schalk's finest realization of a text in song.

A look into the creative process behind this hymn reveals that the crafting of its text was truly a collaborative work between hymnist and composer, with a startling outcome.

The first three stanzas of Vajda's four-stanza hymn read in his original version:

1. Where shepherds lately knelt
   And kept the angel's word,
   I come in half belief,
   A pilgrim strangely stirred,[171]
   But there is room
   And welcome there
   For me.

2. In that unlikely place
   I find him as they said:
   Sweet newborn babe, how frail!
   And in a manger bed,
   A still, small voice
   To cry one day
   For me.

3. How should I not have known
   Isaiah would be there,
   His prophecies fulfilled?
   With pounding heart I stare:
   A child, a son,
   The Prince of Peace
   For me.

Schalk arrived at the soaring structure of his tune by means of two epiphanies.

One was to compile Vajda's shorter phrases into a rising series of three long-arching phrases of the kind he loved to work with.[172] The last takes a poignant turn upward to D-sharp, a gesture that seems to bear within its brief span all the world's longing and hope, before returning to complete the phrase.[173] In this way the two pairs of six-syllable lines become two 12-syllable phrases, and Vajda's three short phrases or 4, 4 and 2 become a 10-syllable phrase:

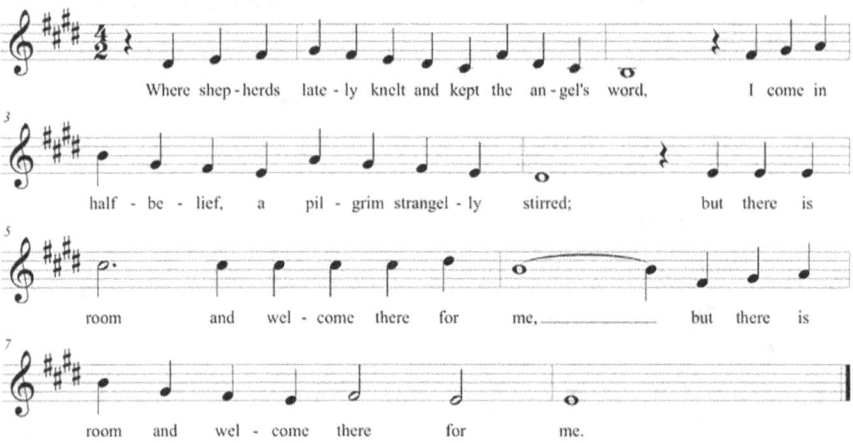

The second epiphany was to repeat that entire 10-syllable phrase. "I asked [Vajda] if I could do that, because I had a certain musical solution." Vajda, who virtually never allowed for any alterations of his texts once they were completed, agreed.[174]

But Schalk had a hand in the final product in another way. As imaginative as Vajda's concept for the text was, a minor adjustment suggested by Schalk to the text in the last stanza changes everything.

Vajda's original version reads, with markings by Schalk indicating emphasis:[175]

> Can I, will I forget
> How Love was born and burned
> Its way into my heart:
> Unasked, unforced, unearned,
> To live and die,
> And not alone
> For me?
>
> Jaroslav J. Vajda
>
> July 9, 1986

Schalk, pondering the last two lines, suggested this revision:

> 4. Can I, will I forget
> how love was born, and burned
> its way into my heart
> unasked, unforced, unearned,
> to die, to live, and not alone for me,
> to die, to live, and not alone for me?

This seemingly minor emendation changes everything. Vajda's first three stanzas draw us poetically into the perspective of a pilgrim tardily arriving at the manger bed, who wonders what this great event means to him. This revision of the final stanza, however, takes us in one sweeping gesture from Christ's birth to his death and resurrection. As we sing, we affirm the birth of the new self in Christ from the ashes of the old self bound in Satan's chains. We find ourselves proclaiming the Christian hope that is the ground for our faith.[176]

Vajda rarely allowed any changes to be made to completed hymn texts.

"The original text of the last stanza ends: 'To live and die, but not alone for me,'" Schalk recalled. "At some point I said, OK, but I think it makes more sense theologically to say 'to die, to live. . . .'" To Schalk's surprise, Vajda agreed. "That *never* happened otherwise with Jary Vajda," Schalk said.[177]

The hymn appears in this emended form in all published versions. But the choir of Grace Lutheran Church, River Forest, where for many years Schalk served in music ministry alongside Paul Bouman, first sang Schalk's anthem setting of this hymn in the original version:

"Where Shepherds Lately Knelt,"
the penultimate of Schalk's manuscript score,
with the original version of Vajda's stanza 4[178]

A letter dated September 1, 1986, from Vajda to Leonard Flachman, then Product Development Director for Augsburg Publishing House, is revealing.

Carl and I are both pleased that you like our Christmas carol, "Where Shepherds Lately Knelt." However, before you set any type, I want to ask you to consider the enclosed version of the text. You will note that I have dropped the capitalization of each line and have opted for lower case in the beginning of a new sentence. I think this will facilitate Carl's handling of the enjambments, where he can pull second and third lines together in stanzas three and four, and also make the first four lines fit two lines of music.

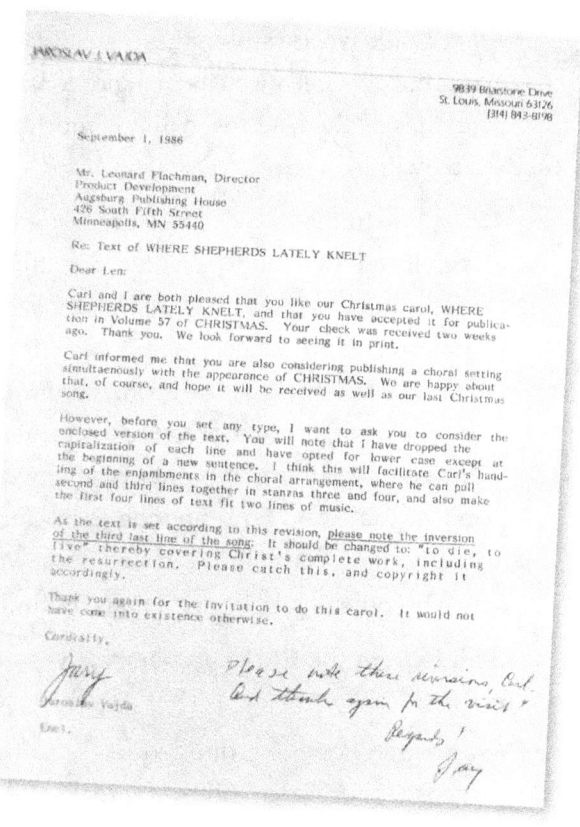

As the text is set according to this revision, <u>please note the inversion of the third last line of the song:</u> It should be changed to "to die, to live," thereby covering Christ's complete work, including the resurrection. Please catch this, and copyright it accordingly.[179]

Conclusion

Living and dying, dying and living: It appears to the naked eye as a simple change in word sequence, but the semantic meaning is deep. The first represents the "human point of view" that Paul tells us we cast off in our new lives in Christ; the second represents our re-orientation in Christ. As Paul writes in 2 Corinthians 5:

> For while we are still in this [earthly] tent, we groan under our burden, because we wish not to be unclothed but to be further clothed, so that what is mortal may be swallowed up by life.
>
> . . . For the love of Christ urges us on, because we are convinced that one has died for all; therefore all have died. And he died for all, so that those who live might live no longer for themselves, but for him who died and was raised for them. From now on, therefore, we regard no one from a human point of view; even though we once knew Christ from a human point of view, we know him no longer in that way. So if anyone is in Christ, there is a new creation: everything old has passed away; see, everything has become new! (2 Corinthians 5:4 and 14-17).

So it is from the Christian perspective, as elegantly expressed by Bouman:

> Christian hope is grounded in Jesus, the crucified Christ, whose offering of himself breaks the power of death, because death cannot render the offering meaningless. Instead, in the resurrection, it is *death* that loses its former meaning as "the end of hope." Christian hope is, therefore, in the triumph of life over death, the triumph of the Spirit of God over the spirit of the demonic.[180]

Let us die to live so that we, with Senfl, Luther, Schalk, and Bouman, may proclaim the works of the Lord in all that we do.

Biography
The Rev. Dr. Walter R. Bouman[181]

July 9, 1929 – August 17, 2005

Walter R. Bouman, the Edward C. Fendt Professor Emeritus of Systematic Theology at Trinity Lutheran Seminary, died August 17 surrounded by family at his home in Columbus. He was 76.

Bouman was a member of the seminary faculty from 1971 until his retirement in 1999. He continued to teach classes as professor emeritus until April 2005, when he was diagnosed with advanced colon cancer.

His popularity as a teacher and guest lecturer crossed all denominations. He preached or taught in more than a hundred Ohio congregations, including Lutheran, Episcopal, United Church of Christ, Presbyterian, Baptist, and Roman Catholic churches. Each year since 1985 he led a group from Broad Street Presbyterian Church in Columbus to Stratford, Ontario, Canada, to attend and discuss the theological significance of Shakespeare's plays. He served as "theologian-in-residence" for the Episcopal Diocese of Southern Ohio during the 2003-04 academic year, and on October 31, 2003, he provided the commentary for a hymn festival at St. Mary's Roman Catholic Church in Port Washington, Wisconsin, to celebrate the Joint Declaration on the Doctrine of Justification.

A devotee of classical music and the hymns of the church, he frequently provided commentary for Lutheran hymn festivals,[182]

Bouman long will be remembered as a leader in the Lutheran-Episcopal dialogues that eventually led to a formal agreement known as *Called to Common Mission*, a relationship of full communion between the Evangelical Lutheran Church in America (ELCA) and the Episcopal Church U.S.A. He was a member of Lutheran-Episcopal Dialogue III from 1983-1991 and the co-drafter of its documents, and was a member of the Anglican-Lutheran International Commission from 1985-1997 and the co-drafter of its documents. He was a consultant to the Anglican-Lutheran Dialogue in Canada, which led to a full communion agreement, and to the conversations between the Anglican churches of Britain and Ireland and the Scandinavian and Baltic Lutheran Churches, which led to the Porvoo Agreement.

He frequently served as visiting faculty at various seminaries and colleges, including the Lutheran Theological Seminary at Gettysburg; the Lutheran Theological Seminary in Philadelphia; Concordia Theological Seminary, St. Louis; The General Theological Seminary, New York City; Luther Theological Seminary, Adelaide, Australia; and the Lutheran theological seminaries of Tokyo and Kobe, Japan. In 2002, he was the Eric Gritsch Theologian-in-Residence at the Melanchthon Institute in Houston, Texas.

Bouman was a member of the American Academy of Religion and the Association of Lutheran Church Musicians, and was a past president of The Lutheran Academy for Scholarship. He was author or co-author of twelve books, including *We Believe*, a book of reflections and prayers on the Augsburg Confession (1999). Of this one reviewer wrote, "It is short and sweet and sound. It is well-packaged and reader-friendly. In fact, it should be sold wherever good medicine is dispensed."[183]

Bouman also contributed to three encyclopedias and ten books, including *Exploring and Proclaiming the Apostles' Creed*, and he was the author of more than 200 journal articles, reviews, audiotapes, and courses on videotape.

The son and grandson of Lutheran pastors, Walter Bouman was born in Springfield, Minnesota, on July 9, 1929. In 1957 he married Janet Gunderman, also a native of Minnesota. Bouman earned his Master of Divinity degree from Concordia Seminary, St. Louis, in 1954 and served congregations in Chatfield, Minnesota, and Albany, New York. In 1963 he earned a doctor of theology degree *magna cum laude* from the University of Heidelberg and received an honorary doctor of divinity degree from The General Theological Seminary, New York, in 1993.

Bouman was known for his humor and rarely started a lecture or classroom discussion without a joke. He loved the music of the church and was instrumental in the formation of a church music program at Trinity. He was invited to give the keynote address at the Constituting Convention of the Association of Lutheran Church Musicians ("Sing to the Lord a New Song: Music and the Mission of the Church," reproduced in the appendix of this volume). For several years he donated his honoraria from speaking engagements and lectureships to a fund for the establishment of a chair in church music at the seminary.

In more recent years, Bouman became an outspoken opponent of the war in Iraq and the death penalty, and a proponent of church blessings for same-sex couples and the ordination of openly gay and lesbian candidates for ministry. More than anything he loved and honored the gospel and the church to which he was called to serve. He was a member of Redeemer Lutheran Church in Columbus.

He is survived by his wife, Jan; sons Andrew (Holly Halligan) of Oakland, California, Luke (Kathy) of Valparaiso, Indiana, and Greg (Dawn) of Cincinnati; grandchildren Kenneth, Janelle, and Nathan; brother David (Lorene) Bouman of Ft. Wayne, Indiana, and sister Trudy (Jay) Decker of Coupeville, Washington; and many nieces and nephews. He was preceded in death by his brother Robert (Kayoko) Bouman.

Afterword

Family remembrances of Walter R. Bouman

Read by his son, Andy Bouman, at the Mass of the Resurrection

Walter Richard Bouman (1929-2005)
Trinity Lutheran Seminary, August 23, 2005

My father was a man with strong opinions. If you've ever been on the receiving end of one of his opinions, you know how vehement he could be about expressing them.

His views about this memorial service were no exception. He left detailed instructions (four pages, single-spaced), including not only requests for the beautiful music we've heard this afternoon, but also a request that one of his sons provide a few words of personal biography. So here are some things you may know, and some things you may not know, about my father's life.

Walter Richard Bouman was born on July 9, 1929, in Springfield, Minnesota, where his father was a Missouri Synod Lutheran pastor.

One of my dad's earliest memories of the parsonage in Springfield was the piano in the living room. It was his mother's pride and joy, and she often played it for my dad and his two younger brothers, Robert and David. She gave my dad his first piano lessons. By the time he was eleven, he had also learned to play the organ from his school principal. He sometimes was the organist for my grandfather's church services.

Growing up in rural Minnesota during the Great Depression, and later the Second World War, my dad and his family didn't have many of the comforts we take for granted. His second home, near Wood Lake, Minnesota, had no central heating. Only two rooms, the kitchen and the dining room, had stoves, so my dad and his two brothers shared a bed in the dining room on cold Minnesota winter nights. There were no indoor toilets. Taking a bath was an all-day affair on Saturdays, as my grandmother heated water continuously on the wood-burning kitchen stove.

My dad was nine years old when rural electricity came through in the fall of 1938. The congregation built a new parsonage, and the family finally had central heating, indoor plumbing, an electric stove, a refrigerator, and a radio. My dad thought it was so wonderful that he imagined heaven would begin with workmen putting up huge poles and stringing wires so there would be electricity for the people in heaven.

The radio expanded my dad's world in significant ways. On Sunday afternoons, the family sat in the living room listening to concerts of the New York Philharmonic Orchestra broadcast from St. Olaf College and the University of Minnesota. My dad also became a fan of the St. Louis Cardinals, the only baseball team whose games were broadcast on the radio in their county.

In 1945, three years after my grandparents adopted my dad's sister Trudy, my grandfather accepted another call, and the family moved to Ft. Wayne, Indiana. A few months later, when my dad was only sixteen, his mother passed away suddenly two days after major surgery. This tragedy had a profound impact on my dad's life. Although my grandfather remarried two years later, my dad spent little time at home after my grandmother's death. He went off to boarding schools to finish high school and junior college.

My dad graduated from Concordia Theological Seminary in St. Louis in 1954. It was, of course, an all-male institution. At that time, there were no female students, seminary professors, pastors, or bishops in any Lutheran churches in this country.

He then headed off to Heidelberg University in Germany on a Fulbright Scholarship for three years of post-graduate study, eventually

Afterword

earning his doctorate in 1963. While he was in Germany, he toured Europe on his holidays and spent some of his leftover fellowship money on some prized possessions, including a set of four wooden recorders (soprano, alto, tenor, and bass) and a harpsichord.

Returning to Minnesota, he was ordained on December 16, 1956. About this time, he also met my mother, Janet Gunderman, who was a teacher at the parochial school at my grandfather's church. They were married in her home church at Fulda, Minnesota, on August 17, 1957. For the next few years, my dad served as the pastor of Lutheran churches in Chatfield, Minnesota (where I was born), and Albany, New York (where my brother Luke was born).

My father began his academic career in 1963, when he received a call to teach theology at Concordia College, a Lutheran college in River Forest, Illinois, an older suburb of Chicago. This was where my youngest brother Greg was born and where my parents bought their first house, a tiny home in Elmwood Park, another Chicago suburb.

I have vivid memories of that house in Elmwood Park. It was here that my dad began his life-long practice of inviting large groups of

The Bouman family in 1974: Luke, Walter, Greg, Janet, and Andy.

students, faculty, family, and friends to our backyard for cookouts. My dad loved to host cookouts. And you always had to compliment him on his cooking. Behind the scenes, my mom spent hours preparing side dishes and cleaning up.

We had a constant succession of people living with us in that house. To help pay the mortgage, my parents rented out the largest bedroom— the one intended to be the master bedroom— to students from Concordia College. (Meanwhile, my brothers and I shared bunk beds in the smallest bedroom.) They also provided improvised bedroom space in the basement to friends and relatives who had little money of their own.

To supplement his modest professor's salary, my father also served as an interim pastor and supply preacher at a number of Chicago area Lutheran churches. We would all go along with him in my parents' car, a VW bug.

My dad's love of cocktail parties was legendary. This was a sophisticated habit that he acquired, I believe, in the early 1950s while he was on his seminary internship in New York City. I learned at an early age to mix a martini and a manhattan. My dad always liked unsalted peanuts with his drink. We never traveled far from home without a minibar packed into a box in the trunk of the car. Whenever we went— Holden Village, church conferences, family celebrations—everyone knew where the party would be: in my dad's room.

During the 1960s, my dad also had early ecumenical contacts that set the stage for his later work on Lutheran-Episcopal dialogue. He was an exchange professor at Rosary College, a Roman Catholic women's college also located in River Forest, Illinois.

In 1971, my father came to teach here at the Lutheran seminary in Columbus, and for the rest of his academic life, this seminary has been his theological and spiritual home. My parents bought their second house, the home on Millerdale Road where they have lived for the past thirty-three years, where my brothers and I finished growing up, and where my father spent his final months after being diagnosed with colon cancer in April of this year.

Afterword

I'd like to finish by sharing a few personal memories of my father.

My dad was an insatiable reader and loved to buy books. He never passed a bookstore without buying something. Eventually, five rooms in my parents' house had wall-to-wall bookshelves.

Along with the theological books, my father loved mysteries, including the Adam Dalgliesh series by British writer P.D. James. He always read the last chapter of a mystery first. He had a long theological justification for this habit, but I always thought he was just impatient to know how the story turned out.

Going for a drive in the car with my dad was always an adventure. Before Holly and I got married twenty-five years ago, we traveled with my family to Indiana to celebrate my grandmother's birthday. Holly was very impressed that my brothers and I all sat in the back seat and allowed her the place of honor with my mom and dad in the front. She didn't realize that we were all terrified of my dad's driving and couldn't stand to watch.

He loved playing games. And he hated to lose. He used to play chess with me after dinner. I soon learned that if I didn't let my dad win the game, he would keep insisting on playing "just one more" until he won one.

He also loved card games, especially bridge. He was a confirmed risk taker. He always bid too high and sometimes actually made his bids, much to the amazement of his more timid partners.

My father loved eating at fine restaurants. In his head he carried around a mental list of his most memorable meals, and could actually quote extensive menus from his all-time favorite meals dating back to 1955.

He also loved live theater. For over twenty years, he accompanied a tour group every August from Broad Street Presbyterian Church here in Columbus to Ontario, Canada, for the Stratford Festival. Over the years, he encouraged many family members and friends to join him on these annual pilgrimages.

My dad loved gardens. He enjoyed walking around and smelling the flowers.

He also loved crossword puzzles. Until the last few days of his life, he always started every day by completing the daily crossword puzzle in the newspaper. Sometimes when he got stuck on a particularly tough clue, he would call my brother Greg for advice. "I need to talk to Greg" was often the urgent way he started these phone calls when someone else answered the phone.

When my dad was younger, he loved to participate in sports. He played softball and volleyball, went jogging, and even rode his bike off to the seminary when the weather was nice. When we lived in the Chicago area, he even participated in a bowling league. He often took us kids along to the bowling alley, so my mom could have some peace when she went back to school.

He loved making detailed plans, especially for trips. "What's the plan?" was one of his favorite questions. We learned early that we better have one, because if we didn't, he'd have one for us.

He had an endless curiosity about the world. He once said that if he hadn't become a theologian, he would have been a scientist.

He never lost his sense of humor. Even during this last illness, he never stopped cracking jokes.

The Bouman family in 1997.

Afterword

He remained a Cardinals fan to the very end. On his last night alive, my cousin Brita, who was sitting up with him, asked him if he wanted to hear the score of the Cardinals game. She wasn't sure if he even heard her. Then she teased him by asking if he wanted to hear the score of the Cubs game. My dad smiled and shook his head no.

My dad adored his grandchildren Ken, Nathan, and Janelle. They were truly the delight of his retirement years. His one regret was that he would not live to see them grow to maturity.

My dad continued to love music all his life. When he was a young man, he spent a good part of his savings from a summer job to buy season tickets to the symphony for his parents. In later life, he was a season ticket holder and patron of the Columbus Symphony Orchestra. He also encouraged the seminary to hold choral evensong services and donated the timpani used in the service this afternoon.

I can think of no more fitting tribute to his memory than the chair in church music that the seminary is establishing in honor of my dad and mom. It was music that comforted him in his final months. And it was through music that he always found the greatest expression of his own strong faith.

APPENDIX

Selected unpublished writings by Walter Bouman

Partners in Proclamation
Pastors and Musicians
A Theologian's Perspective

Association of Lutheran Church Musicians
Region III Conference
Dubuque, Iowa
July 24-27, 1988

You may be tempted to regard the three presentations of the theme of this conference [theologian, pastor, musician] as some kind of smorgasbord from which to pick and choose. Despite Oscar Wilde's assertion that he could resist anything but temptation, resist! Theologian, pastor, musician are not alternatives, but perspectives. The emphasis in my sub-theme is not on "A" theologian, the one among many who happened to be available on this last week in July. Rather, I hope to provide *theological* (in distinction from pastoral and musical) perspective on the theme.

The theme itself, "Partners in Proclamation," would not have been my way of formulating the relationship between pastors and musicians. The concept of proclamation suggests, initially at least, that worship is basically preaching, a function understood to belong to the pastor. Traditionally, the musician has been cast in a role that was subordinate to the function of preaching. When we then seek to upgrade the ministry of the musician, we turn to the word "partner" instead of "subordinate." But we have not challenged the understanding that worship is basically delivering and hearing a sermon. Such an understanding will not help us at all because neither worship nor music is essentially about preaching. (This sound as if I am denigrating preaching, but I want to assure you that I am always edified by good preaching, that I work hard at preaching when that ministry is required of me, and that I have no intention of attacking the importance of preaching in the Christian assembly.)

However, all is not lost. "Partnership" can be a valuable way to describe the relationship of the multiple ministries which ought to be evident in Christian worship. And if "proclamation" is understood as that which the church announces by its being and doing as well as by its words, then it can focus our attention helpfully on an important dimension of Christian worship. Not only is the church called to be a witness that something decisive has happened to the world. But also whenever we eat the bread and drink the cup of the eucharist, we *proclaim* the Lord's death until ee comes (1 Corinthians 11:26).

Nevertheless, I want to say this as strongly as I can: uniquely Christian worship is doing the eucharist. That alone is the appropriate liturgy of people who believe that Jesus is the Christ. Doing anything other than the eucharist means that we are, in fact, still "synagogue," that we are not "church." I hasten to add that being "synagogue" does not mean we have ceased to be "people of God." But it does mean that we are the pre-eschatological people of God, we are people of God as if Jesus were not yet the Christ.

I put it this strongly because I believe that we have to stop deceiving ourselves theologically. I believe that the Christ has come, that Jesus of Nazareth is the Christ. The way I believe this in the gathering of the community is to participate in the eschatological meal, the eucharist. If we do not have the eucharist on a Sunday morning I am deprived of my opportunity to witness that Jesus is the Christ. I cannot be what I am called to be, what all of us who are baptized into Jesus, the Christ, are called to be.

I would like to assume that the normal liturgy of the Lutheran congregation gathered on Sunday is the eucharist, the Holy Communion as proposed and intended to be done by the *Lutheran Book of Worship*. If

I could assume that, the rest of our time this evening could be spent on attention to the relationship between pastor and musician in the context of that normal liturgy. But, like all of us, I am quite aware that for 75-80 percent of the congregations of the Evangelical Lutheran Church in America the eucharistic liturgy cannot be assumed as normal. Perhaps that is just as well for purposes of this lecture. For it requires that we ask once again *why* it is that the eucharist is the normal Sunday liturgy of the gathered congregation. And it is in the context of asking and appropriately answering that question that we can reflect *theologically* on the ministries of pastor and musician and their relationship to each other.

The Development of the Liturgical Assembly in the Apostolic Era

A. Whenever we ask *why* the eucharist is the normal Sunday liturgy of the gathered congregation, we should not ever want to avoid the documents of our apostolic scriptures, what we have come to call the New Testament. And there are good materials available for looking at the New Testament, by Gerhard Delling (*Worship in the New Testament,* 1962) and Ferdinand Hahn (*The Worship of the Early Church,* 1973) among others, as well as chapters in all the standard books on the history of liturgy. But we must not look to the apostolic scriptures for rubrics like those available to us in the LBW or descriptions like those we find in Justin Martyr and Hippolytus, and in their absence conclude that we can do whatever we want. Nor must we imagine that there is a general definition or pattern of worship to be perceived in human religion and then turn to the apostolic scriptures for its particular expression in Christian communities. Nor must we begin with our present forms for worship and seek to validate them anachronistically in the apostolic scriptures.

It cannot be said often enough or strongly enough that Jesus was not the "founder" of a religion to which we happen to or want to belong. Jesus was not even the "founder" of Christianity, one who gave it its doctrines, rituals, and ethos. We have learned in this century to ask in chastened and sober fashion what Jesus was and intended historically, what actually happened in the communities of disciples that came into existence as a consequence of his mission and ministry. This does not mean that we should attempt to repristinate romantically a kind of apostolic "golden age." There was and continues to be development after and out of the matrix of Jesus and the early apostolic communities. But attention to the matrix enables us to discriminate, to ask the question of authenticity as we look at the various developments, and above all to get a fix on the direction in which we ought to be moving.

B. We must begin with the fundamental confession of the apostolic scriptures. It is deceptively simple: Jesus is the Christ, the Messiah. Jesus has been raised from the dead. These are not alternatives. These are two ways of saying the same thing. The resurrection of Jesus from the dead is the starting point of Christian confession. Both are "eschatological" in character. We will not understand what took place in the assemblies of Jesus' disciples unless we grasp that fundamental fact.

"Eschaton" means "end" in the sense of goal or outcome or consummation of history. What the followers of Jesus experienced when they were encountered by Jesus after his execution and burial was not resuscitation or, in the term used by Edward Schillenbeeckx, "reanimation." That would have meant that Jesus returned to the same mode of existence that was his prior to death, that he resumed his life where it had left off. That was indeed the expectation of many pious Jews, that righteous martyrs, unjustly deprived of the fullness of life, would return to live the appropriate length of days. What the disciples encountered was infinitely more awesome. Jesus had been raised to the "eschaton," to the final future of the kingdom of God. That is the significance of the appearances and disappearances that are not subject to the limitations of space and time. That is finally the significance of Luke's "ascension." Jesus does not go to some "place" within the cosmos. He ascends into the future, and he is therefore not "gone." For he is present with and to his disciples in the power of the future. Luke's Acts of the Apostles is not the story of the community *after* Jesus, but rather the story of the community *under* Jesus.

When the disciples encountered Jesus raised as the eschatological Messiah, ascended to the final future of the kingdom of God, present as the power of the future, they were called to radical revision of their relation both to the past and to the future. They were required to re-envision the future and to re-appropriate the past. With regard to the past, the resurrection of Jesus meant that his claim to embody, represent and inaugurate the kingdom of God was indeed valid. His death by execution on the cross was not God's repudiation of his ministry. It was rather the consummation of his ministry. His mission to renew Israel, gather its "lost sheep," and open it to the Gentiles was, in fact, God's mission. His teaching was not blasphemy. It was, in fact, the Word that effected what it announced. His signs were not done by the devil, but they pointed to the fact that the kingdom of God had indeed "come among you." The cross was to be both the way and the consequence of discipleship. Hence the past was to be re-appropriated as the disciple communities retold the stories of Jesus with the "aha" of insight.

But even more radically, they were required to re-envision the future. The resurrection meant that Jesus had (and has) death ultimately and definitely behind him. "Death no longer has dominion over him" (Romans 6:9). That means the future belongs to him. He can make unconditional promises to us. The kingdom of God, not the reign and power of death, will have the last word. This is what led the church to the eventual conclusion that Jesus is God. For if "God" means whatever has the last word in history, then Whatever or Whoever raised Jesus from the death is "God." And because Jesus has been raised from the dead, he now defines and determines what we mean by God. He and the "Abba" whose mission he embodied and the Spirit of the kingdom's future through whom history receives its direction and goal are now the "name" by which God is finally known.

What this means is that something has happened to the world. The power of death has been broken. The world is no longer the same. When it acts as if death still has the last word, it is acting in "bad faith." All the powers of the "old age" operate on the basis of death. They have power because they deal in death. The have power because they threaten death. The "old age" measures power in terms of what can dispense death. We participate in the reign of death, live under the "old age," whenever we enjoy benefits at the expense of others because we can threaten more dispensation of death. We "trust" the powers of death whenever we engage in self-defense, self-aggrandizement, or self-hatred. We trust the powers of death whenever we oppress, exclude, exploit, or destroy others. We trust the powers of death whenever we denigrate, deprecate, or destroy ourselves. We trust the kingdom of God whenever we live as if there were more to do with our lives than preserve them. We trust the kingdom of God whenever we live as if there were more to do with our lives than destroy them. To believe the resurrection of Jesus changes the way we participate in the world. To believe the resurrection of Jesus is to see through the powers of death, to recognize that they are passé, and therefore to be free of their domination. Hence the ultimate *martyria*, the ultimate witness, is the freedom to suffer death because one knows that death does not have the last word.

C. Jesus' mission was the renewal of Israel so that it could fulfill its function in the eschatological triumph of the kingdom of God. Israel was to be the focus for the gathering of the Gentiles. Jesus suffered the cross because of his mission to Israel and to its future for the Gentiles. Hence he died for, on behalf of, the world. But he did not die in order to found a new religious community. His death was not the repudiation of Israel. It was rather God's final, total commitment to Israel. Gerhard Lohfink's dramatic insight is that the "many" for whom his "blood of the covenant" is "poured out" is a reference "first of all to Israel itself, just as the (new) covenant must first refer to Israel."

> Jesus . . . understood his death as a salvific act of God who heals what unbelieving Israel did to him. Israel's dreadful deed would be to overcome, and the people's path to repentance would once again be open. Those who had ruined their lives through their hardening against Jesus re-

ceive from God, freely and without merit, the possibility of a new life (in biblical terms, atonement). God transforms the murder of his emissary into a deed of his *faithfulness* to Israel (in biblical terms, covenant); he turns the death of his emissary, planned and brought about by men, into the establishment of *definitive and irrevocable* faithfulness to Israel (in biblical terms, the new covenant) and thus preservers his claim on the chosen people of God. (Gerhard Lohfink, *Jesus and Community*, p. 25)\

Hence the earliest disciples of Jesus simply announced to Israel and within Israel that Jesus was/is the Christ, the eschatological Messiah. Luke uses the words of the prophet Joel to interpret what happened in the Pentecost experience. Joel simply says, "It shall come to pass *afterwards*" (Joel 2:28). Luke pointedly introduces the Joel quotation with an eschatological formula:

And *in the last days* it shall be, God declares, that I will pour out my Spirit upon all flesh, and your sons and your daughters shall prophesy, and your young men shall see visions, and your old men shall dream dreams; yea, and on my menservants and my maidservants in those days I will pour out my Spirit; and they shall prophesy (Acts 2:17-18).

The gift of the Spirit to all flesh, and not just to chosen individuals, is a mark of the messianic age.

Paul, among others, drew the conclusion that if Jesus was/is the Messiah, if the messianic age has truly come, then Gentiles are to be gathered to the people of God. If Jesus is now "the Way," the Torah, then to be baptized into Jesus replaces both Torah (Galatians) and the "old age" powers of death (Colossians). Jews and Gentiles together witness by their being one people that the messianic age has begun (Romans, Ephesians).

D. The significance of this for the assemblies of the apostolic communities can now be made clear. We can now reconstruct the development of the communal rituals in the following way. The Jewish disciples of Jesus continued to participate in the life of the synagogue and, when in Jerusalem prior to its destruction in 70 C.E., in the rituals of the temple. Paul also goes first to the synagogue whenever he comes to a new city, and he maintains his commitment to the temple until the end.

Simultaneously, however, the disciples of Jesus assembled in homes for that ritual which identified them uniquely: the meal. We find both features in the same passage in Acts: "And day by day, attending the temple together and *breaking bread in their homes*, they partook of food with glad and generous hearts, praising God and having favor with all the people" (Acts 2:47). Obviously, not all Jews, not even the majority of Jews, believed that Jesus was the Christ, the Messiah. But those who did were identified by the ritual which Luke now calls "the breaking of the bread," a phrase which Joachim Jeremias has correctly recognized as a technical term for eucharist. This is significant because the meal was understood to be a characteristic of the messianic age. If Jesus was indeed the Messiah, and if the messianic age had begun, then they would witness to and participate in this fact, this messianic event, by being at the messianic banquet table.

Initially, then, the "worship" of the disciples of Jesus was: participation in the scriptures, exposition, and prayers of the synagogue (and/or temple) in common with all Jews; participation in this messianic age inaugurated by Jesus through the common meal for those baptized into Jesus in private homes. Initially there was a thanksgiving with bread before a regular meal and a thanksgiving with the cup after the meal. Robert Jenson continues the description:

> In Paul's Corinth we see that the first blessing has migrated to join the second, making a special thanksgiving meal after the regular meal; this order is supposed by the Markan text. Next the two meals became distinct observances, and the two thanksgivings of the thanksgiving-meal were joined into one; we do not know quite when or how these things happened, but they had already occurred in Justin Martyr's congregation by the year 150 (*Christian Dogmatics*, Vol. II, p. 340).

By the end of the first century the break between Jesus' disciples and other Jews became complete. There was no longer a place for Jesus' disciples in the synagogue.

> Between 80 and 90 C.E., members of the Pharisiac party gathered at Jamnia (NW of Jerusalem, 4 miles from the Mediterranean Sea) and carried out a series of reforms that made Pharisiac Judaism normative. In the process they eliminated all competing varieties of Judaism, including the Jewish-Christian. They excluded Jewish Christians by inserting into the liturgy the *Birkath ha-minim*, which included a curse on the *Nosrim* (Nazarenes) (Reginald Fuller and Pheme Perkins, *Who Is This Christ?*).

The place once occupied by the regular meal in the assemblies of the disciples of Jesus was now filled by a synagogue-type service of Scripture and prayer. By the time of Justin (150 C.E.) we have the ritual which he describes (Apol. I, 67):

> On the day which is called Sun-day, all, whether they live in the town or in the country, gather in the same place. Then the Memoirs of the Apostles or the Writings of the Prophets are read for as long as time allows. When the reader has finished, the president speaks, exhorting us to live by these noble teachings. Then we rise all together and pray. Then, as we said earlier, when the prayer is finished, bread, wine and water are brought. The president then prays and gives thanks as well as he can. And all the people reply with the acclamation: Amen! After this the eucharists are distributed and shared out to everyone, and the deacons are sent to take them to those who are absent.

Behind this simple ritual structure and action lies a consistent understanding of Jesus, community, history, and mission which has the meal at its center. Jesus is the eschatological messiah. The community of his disciples understands the messianic age to have begun and anticipates its consummation. Here and now their mission is to bear witness both to what has happened and to what they anticipate. They are identified as messianic community by their participation in the messianic banquet.

The Eucharist as Messianic (Eschatological) Banquet

A. Such an understanding of the eucharist as the ritual which uniquely identifies the communities of Jesus' disciples has its roots deep in the Scriptures of Israel. The basic work supporting this statement was done by Geoffrey Wainwright in *Eucharist and Eschatology* (1971). After tracing the role of the meal in the cultic life of Israel, Wainwright explores the linking of the meal and God's future salvation in the prophets of the exile, Deutero-Isaiah and Ezekiel. According to Isaiah the Lord will feed his people on their homeward journey through the desert (49:9f.) as he fed the people of old in the wilderness (48:21). The nations will come to Israel to share in the blessings of the everlasting covenant (55:1-5). Wainwright calls special attention to the passage in the late Isaianic apocalypse "which is of particular significance for the eucharist; it speaks of a *future* feast for *all peoples*, in a context of *the abolition of death* and *a day of salvation and rejoicing*" (p. 21).

> On this mountain the Lord of hosts will make for all peoples a feast of fat things, a feast of wine on the lees, of fat things full of marrow, of wine on the lees well refined. And he will destroy on this mountain the covering that is cast over all peoples, the veil that is spread over all nations. He will swallow up death forever, and the Lord God will wipe away tears from all faces, and the reproach of his people he will take away from all the earth; for the Lord has spoken (Isaiah 25:6-8).

B. Following the exile, the meal motif in relation to messianic expectation intensifies. The age to come will be an age of plenty. The God who fed the people with manna in the wilderness will feed his people again (2 Baruch 29:8). Wainwright quotes the Midrash Rabbah: "Just as the former deliverer (Moses) made manna descend, so also the latter deliverer (the messiah) will make manna descend" (p. 22). Strong eschatological and messianic expectations came to be attached to the Passover by the time of Jesus (p. 23). "The righteous and elect shall be saved on that day. And with that Son of Man they shall eat and lie down and rise up for ever and ever" (Ethiopian Enoch 62:13-16, Wainwright, p. 24).

C. It takes neither much imagination nor much specialized scholarship to recognize why and how the meal plays such an important role in the teaching and activity of Jesus. The feeding of the multitude is the only incident besides the Passion week narratives which is present in all four Gospels (Matthew 14:13-21; Mark 6:32-44; Luke 9:10-17; John 6:1-15) with additional feedings of multitudes in Matthew 15:32-39 and Mark 8:1-10. In John the feeding is the occasion for explicit messianic reflection (John 6:16-59). Central to Jesus' activity is his table collegiality with "sinners" and outcasts (Luke 15:1-2), and the parables which follow conclude with feasting when the lost is found or restored to the family. Jesus' parables of the kingdom include meal settings (Matthew 22:1-14; Luke 14:16-24). Jesus' sayings pick up the eschatological expectations of Gentiles at the messianic banquet table (e.g. Matthew 8:11). In the last meal with his disciples before his execution, Jesus interprets the bread and cup in terms of his imminent death. But of equal importance, Jesus looks beyond his execution to the eschatological consummation. "I tell you, I shall not drink again of this fruit of the vine until that day when I drink it new with you in my Father's kingdom" (Matthew 26:29 and parallels).

D. It is clear, therefore, why the apostolic communities assembled on the "eighth day" (the eschatological name for the day after the seventh day) and why when they assembled it was for the "breaking of the bread." In the resurrection of Jesus the eschaton had begun. They were at the messianic banquet table. Through their participation in the meal they were identified by the Messiah as the messianic community, the eschatological people of God.

At Corinth, according to 1 Corinthians 11, the more affluent members of the community had refused to share the food and wine they brought for both the regular and the eschatological meal with the poor. Their self-protective refusal meant that their meal was no longer "the Lord's Supper," and they need not bother come together for it. They could just as well stay home and eat, wrote Paul. By their action they were oppressing and humiliating others, and thus they denied their identity as eschatological community. By their inability to engage in self-offering they demonstrated that they were still in the grasp of the power of death. Hence Paul "reforms" them by rehearsing the tradition once again, that the kingdom of God is grounded in the death of Jesus, that is, in self-offering, not self-protection. When they participate in the messianic meal they proclaim the Lord's *death* until he comes. They participate in Christ's way of being for the world (self-offering) by offering themselves to be his body for the world.

Damaging Mutations in the History of the Eucharist

A. The church did not heed Paul. It lost the apostolic understanding of itself as eschatological community. How this came about is too long a story to tell at this point. That it is the reality we face becomes evident in a delightfully wicked "marketing plan" for revitalizing American religion presented by Kansas City advertising executive Jack Cashill to the readers of the *Wall Street Journal*.

> My strategy is to consolidate the various name brands, even the strong flagship brands like Southern Baptist, into one identifiable, Exxon-like entity. The target audience here is Mom, Dad, Butch and Sis—solid suburban Americans who want a little God in their life and a place to go before brunch. And after test-marketing various possibilities, I have decided upon the name *Middle American Christian Church*, or *MacChurch* for ad purposes. I will not be sure of MacChurch's theology until focus groups are run, but I plan on following the promotional path blazed so successfully by Holiday Inn. In other words, this will be your "no surprises" church. When Dad brings the family here, he can be sure that they will not be asked to speak in tongues, handle snakes, or give money to the Sandinistas.

Cashill proposes a "market segmentation" approach for Roman Catholicism: RC Light for post-Vatican II liberals, RC Classic for traditionalists, and RC Free "for those more interested in liberation theology than in Papal Bulls." (Quoted by Wade Clark Roof and William McKinney in *American Mainline Religion*, 1987, p. 229)

One thing must be said about the fate of the eucharist, especially in light of Cashill's "marketing plan," and that is that when the church does not understand itself as eschatological community it has historically assumed a consumer orientation. The eucharist is then no longer eschatological meal but is transformed into consumer goods. In the fourth and fifth centuries the church became a salvation institution. One could be assured of salvation after death so long as one was a consumer of the church's sacraments. Worship responded to minimal questions. What is the least that must be said to consecrate bread and cup, transform it into the product one needs? Just the "Words of Institution," said St. Ambrose, and with his answer the eschatological Thanksgiving was lost to the Western church. How long does one have to stay in order to get the benefit? Just through consecration, was the answer; and the Sanctus bells informed worshipers that they could leave without communion. Does one have to be there at all? Just on days of "obligation," was the answer, and "private masses" proliferated. How often does one have to receive communion? Once a year, said the Fourth Lateran Council in 1215, and delivered Christian piety into the "Easter Rule." Protestants sometimes gave different answers, but they continued to ask most of the same questions. The end result was that in both Protestantism and Catholicism the connection between the church and eschaton, Sunday and eschaton, eucharist and eschaton was no longer understood. The insight of J. J. von Allmen is that Protestants falsify Sunday by not having the eucharist every Sunday; Catholics falsify Sunday by having the eucharist every day. When the eschatological character of church and day and liturgy were lost, clergy were necessary to create and dispense a religious product. Musicians were not necessary at all.

Recovery of Roles, Renewal of Partnership

A. We will not be able to work at partnership between pastors and musicians adequately and responsibly unless and until we let our understanding of the church be informed by the eschatological perspective of the apostolic Scriptures, recover the eschatological meal character of the eucharist, and restore the eucharist as the Sunday liturgy of the people of God.

B. The first role to be recovered is that of the people. The liturgy does not belong to the pastor (nor to the musician). It is what the *people* come together to do because they are and understand themselves to be the eschatological people of God. They come together to rehearse the stories of God by which their communal identity is created, informed and shaped. They come together to offer themselves (and time and possessions) into the service of the kingdom of God. They come together to participate in the eschatological meal which anticipates the final banquet of the Messiah and which therefore shapes their witness in the world. Unless the people of God have responsibility for the liturgy as *theirs*, any partnership between pastor and musician will be perverted. For even at its best such a partnership of pastor and musician would take place as ministry done *to* the people, not ministry done *with* the people.

One of the functions of public books for liturgy is to facilitate the people's ownership of the Sunday liturgy. The people must, of course, be taught, better, must actually teach themselves how to use their book. This is neither difficult nor complicated. A cadre of assisting ministers, all members of the community, can be the structural vehicle through which the people of God exercise ownership of and take responsibility for their liturgy. Indeed, if the study and implementation of the liturgy began with the people, that is, with the cadre of assisting ministers, I could envision them calling upon the pastor and the musician for guidance and instruction. And this would be the initial and foundational expression of the partnership between pastor and musician.

Everything that the community does—stewardship, evangelization, ministries of care, social ministry, ecumenism, education—should and can originate in and be shaped by the Sunday liturgy. Congregational officers should be first and foremost assisting ministers in the Sunday liturgy. It is from among the ministers of the liturgy that the corporate officers should be selected (or elected). One could, of course, reverse this and select assisting ministers from among corporate officers; but that would, in my judgment, be a less appropriate move. It would imply that "corporation" (embodiment) is prior to liturgy, rather than the reverse. But the reverse is most appropriate. *Because* we are made body of Christ (*corpus*) in the liturgy we become corporation (embodiment) and require corporate (embodied) officers.

C. The pastor is the "president" (to use Justin Martyr's term) of the liturgical assembly. The pastor does not do the ministry to the congregation as a group and to its individual members, although that is what we (both clergy and laity) have come to expect. The president is the leadership focus for the ministry of the community. Justin identifies three tasks in the liturgy which constitute the specific contribution of the presiding minister. His brief list is instructive.

First, when the reader has finished, "the president speaks, exhorting us to live by these noble teachings." This description does not qualify as the most profound insight into the meaning of the preaching of the Word of God. But Justin does assign the "word" of the community to the president. He is the principal carrier of the community's "ritual rhetoric," to tell again those stories of God which declare what God has done to the world in Jesus, to explore what it means in our lives that we believe what God has done to the world in Jesus, to expose the ways in which the reign of death in us and in our world still resists and denies what God has done to the world in Jesus.

Second, *after* the bread and wine and water are brought to the table (note that setting the table is not the task of the president), "The president then prays and gives thanks as well as he can." This table-thanksgiving is addressed both to God and to the community. In it, God is reminded of God's promises in such a way that the promises, grounded in Jesus, are now present and available to the community through the participation in the bread and the cup. The thanksgiving concludes with the eschatological invocation of the Holy Spirit, promised and given to all as the "down payment" on the future of the kingdom of God (Ephesians 1:14), so that we live in the future as if it were already ours. Robert Jenson's summary:

> We are to praise God by narrative, transitive remembering of God's saving acts, centered in what happens with Jesus, and by prayer for their fulfillment. And we are to participate in this thanksgiving by sharing bread and a cup (*Christian Dogmatics*, Vol. II, pp. 338-339).

Third, the gifts of those able to give "are collected and handed over to the president. He it is who assists orphans and widows, those who are in want through sickness or for some other reason, prisoners, strangers passing through." The liturgy continues as the president administers the gifts of the community for the sake of the needy, not all of whom as members of the community.

D. There are no similar indications about the role of the musician in Justin. Are we to assume that there is no role for the musician? By no means. Music is implied in the very understanding of the church as the eschatological people of God. For if we are indeed the eschatological people of God, then we have been given the new song. Singing the new song is an *essential* mark of our character as the people of the new age. Providing leadership for the community in singing the new song is the role and task of the musician.

Some of what needs to be said about this ministry must be negative. The ministry of the musician is not derived from that of the pastor, nor is it dependent on or subordinate to that of the pastor. The ministry of music derives from the eschatological character of the gospel. The kingdom of God has begun and is moving in history toward its consummation and final victory. Therefore the church, which is created by the eschatological event of Jesus, *must* sing the new song of the kingdom of God. Chinese Christians, when asked what was worst about the years of the "cultural revolution," replied: "We could not sing." I cannot go into detail here on the significant role which the Scriptures of Israel and the apostolic community assign to song. I did that in the keynote lecture which I gave at the constituting convention of the Association of Lutheran Church Musicians at St. Olaf College in August 1986. But it is clear that the new song belongs essentially to the new age and will be part of the new age for eternity.

Therefore the ministry of the musician is to facilitate the singing of the new song so that the church can be what it is called to be and do what it is called to do. The musician plans how this shall be done in the assembly by composing and by drawing on the compositions of others, by mixing repetition and variety, by facilitating the "conversation" between leaders and congregation, by using a variety of instrumental and vocal soloists and ensembles to supplement and/or support the congregation. The musician plans how this shall be done by taking into account the limitations, abilities, and tastes of the congregation, and also by identifying and utilizing the rich variety of gifts with which God has gifted the congregation, and indeed, the universal church.

E. In the partnership of musician, assisting minister and pastor, the term "partnership" need not mean that all contribute equally or that all have equal responsibilities. I could imagine that rarely would the pastor have basic responsibility for the planning of each Sunday liturgy. A desirable goal would be that musician and assisting minister, working together, would make the final decisions for each Sunday liturgy. The president (pastor) should be consulted, of course. But since the pastor's responsibility is focused in the sermon and the Great Thanksgiving (which should never be reduced simply to the "Words of Institution"), the pastor has little or no responsibility for many of the decisions about the particulars of the rite.

Beginning with the lessons for the day, the musician could select hymns, decide how the psalmody is to be sung, work with the assisting minister to make decisions about the Entrance Rite (not very long on most Sundays) and the liturgical canticles (psalmody, offertory, post-communion hymn). The musician should have responsibility for preparing and "administering" all musical ministers: choirs, soloists, instrumentalists, the chanting of the presiding and assisting ministers, the singing of the congregation.

The assisting minister should plan the prayer of the church, solicit and receive petitionary requests (but not be limited by them), make or preside at announcements, introduce both visitors and the day, read the lessons or work with those who do, preside at the offering and the setting of the table, determine the pattern for distribution (number of stations and ministers needed), administer the cup, choose the post-communion collect, dismiss the congregation. The assisting minister should have responsibility for all the ministries of the gathered people of God: ushers, lectors, acolytes, communion assistants. In everything, it should be clear by what the assisting minister and others do that this is the *congregation's* liturgy.

The focus here has been on the planning and leadership of each individual Sunday's liturgy. I have not said anything about seasonal planning. This might well be the responsibility of a worship committee or an *adhoc* seasonal committee. Pastor, musician, and at least some of the assisting ministers need to be on such worship or seasonal committees *ex officio*. If all of this seems to be too time-consuming, it needs to be remembered that both identity and mission are determined by the eucharistic liturgy of the gathered people of God. Time spent on teaching, planning and preparation for the eucharistic liturgy is not time taken from other tasks, but rather time devoted to and determinative of all other tasks.

The identity and mission of the people of God is communal and requires partnership (Philippians 1:3-11). The basis for the "partnership" must be the shared vision of the gospel as beginning and final triumph of the kingdom of God, the shared vision of the church as *avant garde* of the kingdom of God, the shared vision of the eucharist as the meal which both celebrates and anticipates the messianic banquet. Where such a shared vision informs the ministries of congregation, lay assisting minister, musician and pastor, authentic communal identity and authentic communal mission will bear witness to the vision.

Walter R. Bouman
Columbus, Ohio
July 13, 1988

Sing to the Lord a *New* Song
Music and the Mission of the Church

Constituting Convention
Association of Lutheran Church Musicians
St. Olaf College, Northfield, Minnesota
August 11, 1986

Canticum novum est canticum crucis (Martin Luther).

It is an honor for me to be your guest and to have been invited to give the keynote address for this convention. I am not a musician, and leadership in the church's ministry of music is not my calling. In a sense, that gives me an opportunity to speak to you on behalf of all who have been edified by your ministries, all who are enlisted by you in the mission of making music within the context of Christian worship, all who work with you in the planning and leading of worship, all who have a significant investment in the coming-to-be of this organization because they share in your ministry.

I speak for all of them in wishing you well, in being encouraged by the proposed constitutional purpose of the Association of Lutheran Church Musicians, and in supporting the ministry you represent. You want to establish standards for the ministry of music in the Lutheran church, to facilitate study and growth on the part of all who are engaged in or who are touched by this ministry, to encourage cooperation and trust in the mutual ministry of clergy and musicians, to foster ecumenical experience between musicians in the Lutheran and other Christian traditions. I want to address these purposes this morning because they are worthy of the church's support and response. I want to do this with a focus on the relationship between music and the mission of the church.

I could not discover a great deal of literature on this subject in English language publications. Carl Schalk, editor of *Key Words in Church Music* (Concordia, 1978), has enlisted a number of theologians for brief contributions on the history and theology of church music. Joseph Gelineau has a fine brief statement on the theology and history of "Music and Singing in the Liturgy" in *The Study of Liturgy* (Oxford, 1978). The late Eric Routley has written more prolifically in English than anyone else, most recently by revising an earlier work of his, *Church Music and the Christian Faith* (Agape, 1978). The best lengthy treatment is in German, Oskar Soehngen's "Theologische Grundlagen der Kirchenmusik," *Leiturgia*, Vol. 4 (Johannes Stauda-Verlag, 1961). All of these authors contradict Henry E. Horn's assertion that "music is not essential to worship" (*O Sing to the Lord*, Muhlenberg Press, 1956, p. 9). Indeed, Gelineau calls attention to the fact that music, in contrast to such later developments as the church year, buildings and visual art, belongs to the *universal* elements of Christian worship, present from the beginnings of Christian worship together with Scripture and its proclamation, prayer and the eucharistic meal.

However, despite the universal presence and significance of music, the Lutheran churches in North America have not succeeded in developing the ministry of *"Kantor"* or its equivalent, as have our European ancestral churches. Even where parishes have employed musicians on a full-time basis, the position has had difficulty establishing itself as a ministry. The problem is certainly not the availability of trained and competent musicians. The problem has a lot to do with the American context and with the way Protestant Christianity has come to function in that context.

Over the course of several centuries—give or take a few decades—and through awakenings, camp meetings, revivals, and the success of "frontier religion," two basic "models" of the church became dominant for American Protestantism. The first one I will call the "salvation institution" model. This model offers sinners other-worldly salvation if only they will "accept Jesus as personal Savior" or "make a decision for Christ." Worship has conversion as its basic function. Music tries to portray the joy in store for those who convert—often hand in hand with a world-denying posture. ("I'm but a stranger here; heaven is my home. Earth is a desert drear; heaven is my home.") The sermon ends with an altar call accompanied by music designed to encourage decisions.

The second model I will call the "service institution" model. In this model the clergyperson makes an array of religious services available to a clientele: marriages, baptisms, religious instruction for the young, confirmations, counseling, sick visits, burials. Worship is one of the services (no play on words intended), and it is designed to be attractive and comforting to the clientele, to the people who pay the bills and support the ministry.

In both models the clergyperson is a kind of religious entrepreneur. The clergyperson must gather, hold, maintain and, if possible, increase the membership of a community that is economically viable, a community that is able to own and equip a building, staff and administer a program of worship, education, and pastoral care. The "buck" stops with the clergyperson. If successful, the clergyperson gets the credit; if not, the blame. In both models, staff persons are subordinate to the clergy leader, extensions of clergy leadership, working largely at the will of the clergy leader.

In worship, the clergyperson is cast in a double role as both impresario and star. The clergyperson puts together the "worship experience," and music as well as other aspects of the event are integrated to fit what the clergyperson intends to do to and for the congregation on any given occasion. In the process worship becomes a form of religious entertainment. It must compete with other attractions for the time and attention of the church-goer.

Television religion is thus the quintessential expression of American religion. Television, writes Neal Postmann (*Amusing Ourselves to Death*, Viking, 1985), turns everything it touches into entertainment.

(He entitles his chapter of religious television "Shuffle Off to Bethlehem.") And he asks appropriately whether Christianity—and indeed any religion—can survive being turned into entertainment. The components of warship are determined by their ability to be appreciated by the clientele, to respond to what the clientele finds entertaining, engrossing, what will get and hold attention—in short, what will "play in Peoria." That the consequences have not been fortuitous for the development of authentic ministries of music goes without saying. What needs to be added is that neither the "salvation institution" model nor the "service institution" model represents an authentic vision of the church.

We will not discover an authentic role for music in the Christian community and hence an authentic ministry of music unless and until we can recover a more faithful vision of the church. Of course, as religious philosopher Paul Ricoeur says, an authentic model demonstrates its authenticity in part by its capacity to take up within it whatever is valid from inauthentic models. There is a salvation dimension and a service dimension to Christianity, but both must be taken up into the context of the New Testament vision that the church is "eschatological community."

The New Testament understands the church to be the community that is in on the secret of history itself: that history's outcome is determined by the fact that Jesus of Nazareth is the Christ, the Messiah of Israel. That sentence needs to be unpacked.

For centuries, at least from the time of the Davidic monarchy, Israel anticipated and hoped for a consummation of history which would come about through a messianic king. The Messiah would renew Israel, gathering its "lost sheep" into the fold. The Gentile nations would be drawn to Israel's renewal and witness in a universal era of peace and justice. Even nature would live in reconciled harmony. Such a vision is the content of the new song expressive of the hope of Israel:

> *O sing to the Lord a new song, for he has done marvelous* things!
> His right hand and his holy arm have gotten him victory.

> The Lord has made known his victory, he has revealed his vindication in the sight of the nations.
>
> He has remembered his steadfast love and faithfulness to the house of Israel. All the ends of the earth have seen the victory of our God. Make a joyful noise to the Lord, all the earth; break forth into joyous song and sing praises!
>
> Sing praises to the Lord with the lyre, with the lyre and the sound of melody!
>
> With trumpets and the sound of the horn make joyful noise before the King, the Lord!
>
> Let the sea roar, and al that fills it; the world and those who dwell in it!
>
> Let the floods clap their hands; let the hills sing for joy together before the Lord, for he comes to judge the earth.
>
> He will judge the world with righteousness, and the peoples with equity (Psalm 98).

Jesus of Nazareth announced the good news that in his ministry the final reign of God was breaking out. He was engaged in the renewal of Israel, reconciling and gathering the outcasts and the despised (women, children, tax collectors, lepers), reconstituting the twelve-tribe confederacy in anticipation of drawing the Gentile nations to a universal community of peace and justice. He spread the messianic banquet before the multitudes. He healed the sick and rejoiced the hearts of the bereaved by restoring their loved ones. He fell victim to those who were threatened by the radical vision that he embodied. It seemed as if his claims and expectations were mistaken.

However, after his burial, his disciples began to have experiences of Jesus beyond death. They encountered him, not as someone resuscitated, ready to continue where he had left off. They encountered him as an "eschatological event," that is, as one in whom and through whom the final reign of God had broken out. If they believed what they encountered, then they were in on the secret of history: the new and final age had begun. Death would not have the last word. They were indeed the vanguard of a renewed Israel called to live out the implications of the messianic age. Jesus was indeed the Christ, and he was the Christ not despite the cross but through the cross. He overcame the power of death by becoming its victim. He embodied God's final and irrevocable commitment to the world. The last word would be forgiveness, not revenge. The disciples were called to that vision and confession. They heard the parables of Jesus and they saw the ministry of Jesus as expressions of the final reign of God. They remembered codes such as the "Sermon on the Mount" as the "Torah" of their new community. They listened to exhortations to live out their calling in such apostolic formulations as Ephesians 4—6 and Colossians 3.

Their song was indeed the new song of the messianic age, the age of the breaking out of the final reign of God. They sang the songs of life in the midst of the powers of death, as Paul and Silas did in prison (Acts 16:25). But above all they sang in the context of a renewed worship ritual: the messianic banquet. At his last meal with the disciples (the twelve, the reconstituted Israel), Jesus promised that he would eat and drink anew with them in the breaking out of the final reign of God. They identified themselves as the community of the new age by gathering for the messianic meal. They were carriers of the prophetic vision:

> On this mountain of the Lord of hosts will make for all peoples a feast of fat things, a feast of wine on the lees, of fat things full of marrow, of wine on the lees well refined. And he will destroy on this mountain the covering that is cast over all peoples, the veil that is spread over all nations. He will swallow up death forever, and the Lord God will wipe away tears from all faces, and the reproach of his people he will take away from all the earth (Isaiah 25:6-8).

The meal gave them their identity: end-time or new-age community, and their mission: to bear witness to Jesus was the messiah and to the "secret" that the new age had begun.

The new songs belonged essentially to the new age. One can recognize the new song everywhere in the New Testament. Oskar Soehngen calls attention to the hymnic character of the first chapter of Ephesians and to the two "songs" into which it is divided, Ephesians 1:3-14 and 15-23. More widely recognized are the messianic songs expressive of justice for the oppressed (Luke 1:46-55) and reconciled peace (Luke 1:68-79). The Christ hymn of Philippians 2:5-11 encourages the community in its calling:

> Have this mind among yourselves, which you have in Christ Jesus, who, though he was in the form of God, did not count equality with God a thing to be grasped, but emptied himself, taking the form of a servant, being born in the likeness of men. And being found in human form he humbled himself and became obedient unto death, even death on a cross. Therefore God has highly exalted him and bestowed on him the name which is above every name, that at the name of Jesus every knee should bow in heaven and on earth and under the earth, and every tongue confess that Jesus Christ is Lord, to the glory of God the Father.

Most easily recognized are the hymns which form an early climax in the Revelation of John, with the community gathered on the Lord's Day, with the Lamb in the midst (a reference to the self-offering of Jesus on the cross now present in the eucharistic meal).

The final reign of God is not a flight from the world but rather God's ultimate affirmation of it. Therefore the community sings:

> Worthy art thou, our Lord and God, to receive glory and honor and power, for thou didst create all things, and by thy will they existed and were created (Revelation 4:11).

The death and resurrection of Jesus have disclosed to us the outcome of history, the final triumph of life, and advent of universal peace and justice. The church trusts that vision by its own priestly offering of itself for the world (Romans 12:1-2).

> Worthy art thou to take the scroll and to open its seals, for thou wast slain and by thy blood didst ransom women and men for God from every tribe and tongue and people and nation, and hast made them a kingdom and priests to our God, and they shall reign on earth (Revelation 5:9-10).

Because the reign is from the cross, it will not be tyrannical or oppressive. "I, when I am lifted up from the earth, will draw all persons to myself" (John 12:32).

Here the church is already engaged in the activity which will characterize it forever in the consummation: singing the new song.

> Worthy is the Lamb who was slain, to receive power and wealth and wisdom and might and honor and glory and blessing! . . . To him who sites upon the throne and to the Lamb be blessing and honor and glory and might for ever and ever! (Revelation 5:12-13).

Many dimensions of the church's "existence between the times," between the beginning and the consummation of the new age, will not be needed in the consummation. Special buildings will disappear when the people are the "holy temple." A special temporal cycle (the church year) will not be needed in the midst of secular time. A special ministry within the ministry of the whole people of God will disappear when there will be no need to teach and admonish one another (Jeremiah 31:31-34; Colossians 3:16). But two activities anticipate the consummation: the messianic banquet and the new song. Hence they are so essential to the church's identity (community of the new age) and mission (witness to the breaking out of the new age in the event of Jesus as the Christ).

But is Martin Luther mistaken, then, when he says *canticum novum est canticum crucis*? The whole quotation comes from his Leipzig debate of 1519. "Singing to the Lord does not always mean joyful and happy circumstances. For the new song is the song of the cross. And that means praising God and carrying God with you in the midst of persecutions and in death itself" (*WA* II, p. 333). Here we encounter the true difference between the "new song" of the end-time or new-age community, on the one hand, and religious entertainment, on the other hand. Here we will also see that it was basic differences with regard to what constituted the "new" in the new age that gave the reformers of the sixteenth century such radically different perspectives on the place of music in worship.

Ulrich Zwingli (1484-1531), the Swiss reformer, saw the "new" as the liberation of the "spiritual" from the "material." 1 Corinthians 14:15 was decisive for his approach to worship: "I will pray with the spirit and I will pray with the mind also; I will sing with the spirit and I will sing with the mind also." Zwingli understood "spirit" to refer to mental, not physical, activity, the platonic influence on his outlook. Singing, though not morally wrong at the time, distracts from true worship, true devotion. "In silence the one who prays can best speak to God. Nothing must entice him either through sight or hearing from good devotion." Thus Zwingli forbade all congregational singing from worship in Zurich, and it was not introduced until 1598, sixty-seven years after Zwingli's death.

For Jean Calvin (1509-1564), the French reformer, the "new" in the new age was "maturity" replacing "childhood." "In the childhood stage of the people of God, at the time of the law (*sub legali cultu*), instrumental music was allowed, to attract people to the Word of God; but now we have come to maturity in Christ (Galatians 3:23)". The Evangelical Church Order of Calvinist Lippe declared in 1684 "the organ and other musical instruments and their playing are no piece of Christian worship." Heidelberg had no organs in their churches until 1657; Zurich none until the nineteenth century! Only unaccompanied unison singing was permitted by Calvin. Harmony is a distraction from the Word of God and inappropriate for the presence of God. "I see that one cannot forbid the people all pleasure. It is sufficient that they understand: one permits them what is not actually blasphemous. . . . But there is a great difference between the music with which one enjoys oneself at home or at the table and the Psalms which are sung in the church in the presence of God and the angels." In the last analysis, Calvin was suspicious of music with its mysterious and uncanny power to move people. It had, he said, *use vertu secrete et quasi incredible*. Music was childish, foolish, mysteriously manipulative, and hence it had not place in the maturity which Christ confers on his church.

Martin Luther (1483-1546), the Saxon reformer, had an affirming attitude toward music in worship which is undoubtedly well-known to those in attendance here today. What distinguished Luther from other reformers was that he distinguished "old" from "new" in terms of "bondage" and "freedom." The "bondage" with which he identified the "old age" was the reign of a familiar trio: sin, death and the devil. That puts Luther right in the midst of the thought world of the New Testament. The "old age" is indeed characterized by the powers of death. To live under those powers is to be self-protective, self-justifying. For Luther that is bondage because we cannot bring it off. Justification can only come from the final outcome of history, for only then are the final consequences of my life disclosed. But I am not and cannot be in control of the final outcome. To attempt self-justification is not to trust the One who is Lord of the final outcome of history: Jesus, the crucified and risen Christ. Not trusting Jesus is the essence of sin against God. To engage in self-protection means that I can only postpone the inevitable. I cannot build a final protection against death. To protect myself means that I am not free for my neighbor, especially if that neighbor is an enemy.

When the new age breaks out in the midst of the old age it confers the freedom that comes from believing the promise that life really will have the last word, that the reign of God will triumph over the reign of the powers of death, that forgiveness and not judgment will be God's final verdict upon us, that in Christ God truly does justify us even though we cannot foresee the final justification of our lives and must therefore "sin boldly." This provides a context for Luther's affirmation of all that is creaturely and earthly in the worship of God, including and especially music. The gospel confers freedom, but freedom does not mean having unlimited or at least many possibilities open to us.

Freedom means that we experience our own appropriate creaturely destiny. Hence the creaturely and the material are never the opposite of the "spiritual," but rather the vehicle for the Holy Spirit. The Spirit is not to be understood platonically as escape from the earthly. Rather the Spirit is to be understood eschatologically, that is as the "down payment" on the future of the redeeming reign of God (Ephesians 1:14). "Spiritual songs" therefore have everything to do with content and purpose. We sing the new songs of the new age, that is, living in the future of God's reign of life as if it were already here.

All of this helps us to understand the context for Luther's brief but epigrammatic *Skizze peri tes mousikes*, written at Coburg in 1530:

> I love music, and then enthusiasts who condemn it please me not.
>
> Because it:
>
> 1. is a gift of God, not of humans.
>
> 2. makes me joyful.
>
> 3. chases the devil.
>
> 4. awakens guiltless joy.
>
>> By it are driven out
>>> wrath, anger,
>>>> lusts, pride.
>
>> I give music the first place after theology.
>
>> This derives from the example of David and all the prophets, because they handed on everything that was theirs in meter and song.
>
> 5. it rules in times of peace.
>
>> Stay with it, and humanity will be better off after us on account of this art because it lives in peace. I praise the princes of Bavaria because they cultivate music. Among us Saxons only weapons and bombs are preached.

Luther recognizes, as do all the reformers, that music can be taken into the service of the powers of death. This occurs not only when it is connected with obvious evil, for example, playing string quartets for Jews on the way to the gas chambers to prevent them from guessing the murderous fate toward which they were being marched. Music can also be taken into the service of the powers of death when it perverts the message of the gospel from its authentic content of the triumph of God's reign in Jesus, the crucified and risen Messiah. Music can be taken into the service of the powers of death when it offers false comfort or comforts those who ought to be converted, when it does not give hope or lead the church to give hope to the poor, the oppressed and the defeated. G. K. Chesterton wrote for the church:

> From all that terror teaches, from lies of tongue and pen,
> From all the easy speeches that comfort cruel men,
> From sale and profanation of honor and the sword
> From sleep and from damnation, deliver us, good Lord!
> (*Lutheran Book of Worship,* hymn 428, stanza 2)

Easy hymns as well as easy speeches can "comfort cruel men." Many of our uses of "the sword" in our history as well as in present policies have means that both honor and military power have been sold and profaned.

Now we can begin to understand why *canticum novum est canticum crucis* (the new song is the song of the cross). Because the new age has broken into our history in the midst of the old age, because the powers of death are truly defeated and have become passe but are nevertheless very much with us, we are plunged by out baptism and calling into the struggle between the old age and the new age. The church is the place where the struggle takes place not only because it is called to witness to the breaking out of the final reign of God but also because the battle line between the old and the new runs through each of the baptized. Baptism thus complicates our lives because it calls into question all our tendencies to serve the powers of death with our quest for self-protection and self-justification. The ministry of music is authentic and faithful when it identifies areas of struggle and encourages in the struggle with the vision of the gospel, as Chesterton's hymn does, or

Fosdick's "God of Grace and God of Glory" (LBW 415).

In the last analysis music can be an authentic ministry and parish musicians can function faithfully as Christian ministers when there is a creative and mutually interdependent relationship between music and theology. Theology has as its calling so to listen to the event of Jesus as the Christ mediated to us through the Scriptures of Israel and the canonical documents of the apostolic church that it discerns the good news of the final reign of God and is guided in its life and witness. Music has as its calling the cultivation of a living tradition of sound made by voices and instruments through which the church can be identified as the community of the new age, singing a new song in anticipation of the consummation of the reign of God, encouraging the church in its struggle until the consummation is granted.

If one could describe the optimum parish context, it would be one in which neither clergy nor musicians were doing something to or for the members of the congregation, but where the congregation so believes its baptism that it wants and shares in the vision articulated by theology and served by music, where the ministries of clergy and musicians represent and reflect the vision which the congregation has caught from the gospel. I believe that it is the vision which this association seeks to cultivate. If it does so, it will make clear why Martin Luther identified music as one of the genuine marks of the church. In his treatise on Council and Churches of 1539, Luther said that the church could be recognized by preaching, baptism, the Lord's Supper, forgiveness, calling and ordaining of pastors, and *prayer and the singing of psalms.* "The holy Christian people are externally recognized by prayer, public praise and thanksgiving to God. Rest assured that where there is such singing, here a holy Christian people of God are present." (*LW,* Vol. 41, p. 164).

Cultivating music as a mark of the church is the challenge, calling, and ministry of Lutheran church musicians.

Final Sermon
The Rev. Dr. Walter R. Bouman

Gloria Dei Chapel, Trinity Lutheran Seminary
May 18, 2005
The Holy Eucharist

My thanks to Bexley Hall for the invitation to preach today. It is appropriate because my [Episcopal] colleague Bill Petersen and I worked together on Lutheran-Episcopal Dialogue III and there first dreamed of a relationship between Bexley Hall and Trinity Seminary. My thanks to all of you for your prayers and greetings, your visits and your care, your love and support. I am sustained by the gospel and the eucharist.

(An aside: My pastor, Al Debelak, came to share communion in the hospital. He had the prayers and a lesson, and the great thanksgiving. My roommate had a large, noisy, extended family. And when the first of his family visitors arrived, he said: "Do you know what? They had a mass at the next bed! Isn't that right?" he asked me. I said, "Yes." Then he said, "What are you?" I replied, "A Lutheran." "What are Lutherans?" he asked. "Reformed Catholics," I said. And then as each new family member arrived, he repeated, "They had a mass at the next bed. My roommate is a Lutheran, and they're Reformed Catholics!")

Jan and I are also sustained by the seminary community in its broadest sense. Thank you.

Of course I have turned to some of my favorite jokes about death. Woody Allen: "It is impossible to experience your own death objectively and still carry a tune." "Some things are worse than death. Have you ever spent two hours with an insurance salesman?" Johnny Carson is my favorite so far: "It is true that for several days after you die, your hair and fingernails keep on growing, but the phone calls taper off."

I first thought of preaching on that important holy day this week, *Syttende Mai* [May 17, Norwegian Independence Day (from Sweden) in 1905]. This is also the week of Pentecost, and then we are anticipating the dreaded Trinity Sunday. Before I discovered that the Trinity is the story we tell of God because of the gospel, I thought that I was preaching the incomprehensible to the uncomprehending. But today I want to direct our attention to another word from Scripture, some verses from Psalm 90. The days of our life are seventy years, and perhaps eighty, if we are strong; even then their span is only toil and trouble; they are soon gone, and we fly away. . . . So teach us to count our days that we may gain a wise heart (Psalm 90:10 and 12).

I'm counting. I'm counting. It took a blow to the head with a two-by-four to get my attention. But I'm counting. The oncologist told me I have six to nine months. When do I start counting, I asked him, April 1 or May 1? That's a quibble, he replied. So I haven't exactly begun a countdown. You know, 180 minus 1 and counting. But I am aware that each day is a gift, to be treasured and savored. I am listening to the classical music on WOSU-FM a lot these days. Just listening. Hearing new music and new things in familiar music. I have been thinking that I could happily spend a lot of eternity just listening to music. Bach, above all.

When I first returned home from the hospital I prayed each night that God would not let me wake up in this world. But then Anna Madsen sent me an e-mail saying, "Don't you dare die until I get to Columbus." When Anna talks, even God listens. So I stopped praying the prayer. Instead I have turned to a prayer that I first prayed in German as a child. *"Breit aus die Flügel beide, O Jesu meine Freude, und nimm dein Küchlein ein."* My own rough translation is "Spread out both of your wings, O Jesus, my Joy, and gather in your little cupcake."

Hard now to think of myself as a "little cupcake," so I pray the English translation instead:

> Lord Jesus, who does love me,
> Oh spread thy wings above me,
> And shield me from alarm.
> Though evil would assail me
> Thy mercy will not fail me.
> I rest in thy protecting arm.

But I'm counting.

The purpose for the counting is not like sitting on death row. It is to gain a wise heart, or in an older translation, that "we may apply our hearts unto wisdom." I have been thinking much about what wisdom I have gained, what is of such importance that it must be shared with you today. I have come up with four essentials. I tried to make it a Lutheran three, but these four seemed irreducible.

The first is God's own foolishness, which is wiser than our wisdom.

Who could have imagined that Jesus, the crucified Jew, is the Messiah of Israel and the world? He is identified as Messiah by his resurrection from the dead. The gospel is not an idea, for example, that God loves us, although that is true. The gospel is good news, it is the announcement that something good and absolutely decisive for the universe has happened. The Christian good news is simply "Jesus is risen!" That is good news because it means that death no longer has power over him. Jesus, not death, will have the last word. But the resurrection of Jesus was not personal vindication. He has become the first fruits of all that sleep. For as in Adam all die, so in Christ shall all be made alive. He will reign until he has put all things under his feet. The last enemy to be destroyed is death. And then God will be everything in everyone (1 Corinthians 15:22-28).

Note that this is a vision for the future and it beckons us to follow it. Of course Jesus is also about the past, our past, the world's past. There on the cross he takes sin and evil and death into God's own being and history, where it is overcome forever. But the gospel is first and foremost a vision for the future. Because Jesus is risen, everything has changed radically. We are set free from serving the powers of death with our lives, our fears, our policies. We are set free from having to protect ourselves at whatever cost to others. We are set free from the dreadful necessity to grab all the gusto we can because we only go around once. We are set free from the compulsion to cling to every day and hour of life in this world.

Note also that this vision applies to everyone. Paul says "all" repeatedly, and I take it that he means "all." Robert Farrar Capon taught me some years ago that Jesus did not come to repair the repairable, correct the correctable, improve the improvable. He came to raise the dead! The only final condition for eternal participation in Christ's victory is that we be dead, 100 percent gold-plated dead! Paul exults in God's universal forgiveness. "For God has imprisoned all in disobedience so that he may be merciful to all"(Romans 11:32). It is God's unconditional love that evokes his outburst of praise: "O the depths of the riches and wisdom and knowledge of God. How unsearchable are his judgments and how inscrutable are his ways" (Romans 11:33).

We really have trouble getting it. Ann Lamott quotes the pastor of "The Church of 80 Percent Sincerity:" We are capable of unconditional love, but it has a shelf life of about eight to ten seconds. "We might say to our beloved, 'Darling, I'll love you unconditionally until the very end of dinner.'" It is God's eternal unconditional love that distinguishes God from us (Hosea 11:8-9), and not God's infinity or presumed immortality. Difficult as it is (because I always think of it as unfair), I have come to accept God's universal salvation as the final consequence of the resurrection of Jesus. I think of all: the best and worst, the innocent and the guilty, the victims of the holocaust and the evil perpetrators, those killed in all of our senseless wars, and the misguided leaders who send them into battle. Christ will raise us all, and somehow bend us into shape so that in eternity we become the human beings we were intended to be.

Because Christ is risen, because the messianic age has come, Christ's messianic people are identified by our participation in the messianic banquet.

Nothing has changed so much in my lifetime as the church's understanding of the eucharist. In my youth the eucharist was a penitential ritual, associated with repentance and forgiveness, with confession and absolution. Of course, we are set free to repent by God's unsearchable forgiveness. But as we have begun to recover our roots in Judaism, we have discovered that because the messianic age is here, we are already at the Messiah's feast (Isaiah 25:6-9). This is the feast of victory for our God. Well, it is only hors d'oeuvres on this side of the grave, but it is already a foretaste of the feast to come. This is what identifies us as Messiah's people. When I graduated from seminary fifty-one years ago, I don't think there were 100 Lutheran parishes that had weekly eucharist. Now there are many thousands, and the number grows apace.

So, in Gordon Lathrop's wonderful insight, you are ordained to be table waiters. That is what it means to serve. Ordained ministry is not about meeting people's needs, although that is a dimension of the whole church's ministry to the reign of God. Still less is it about accommodating people's bondage to the powers of death so that we can keep our jobs. Ordained ministry is quite simply that we wait on table, where Christ is already embracing us with his victory, and eating and drinking new with us in the Father's kingdom (Matthew 26:29).

The eucharist also gives us our mission. For what is present to us in this meal is nothing less than Christ's offering of himself for the world. In the meal he takes us up into his offering and makes us his body for the world. In the eucharist we experience that there is more to do with our lives than to protect them. We are set free to offer them. We pray: "We offer with joy and thanksgiving what you have first given us: ourselves, our time, and our possessions." Only Christ can make such a total claim upon us, and only Christ can set us free for such a total offering. So we are free to gather as the church made visible at the table and then free to be sent as the church scattered in total service to the reign of God.

Because Christ is risen, we are free to love the church.

I don't mean the church that gives us warm fuzzies, that embraces us with comfort and love. I mean the real church, the church that fills us with dismay, that robs us of hope, that pursues agendas so contrary to the mind of Christ that we want to despair. That's the church we are free to love. The church that elects a pope who seems unwilling to address the urgent issues facing church and world. The church in Kansas that seems determined to pit Genesis against evolution instead of recognizing that a literalistic interpretation of Genesis has little to do with the origins and meanings of the traditions in Genesis and the place of creation theology in the proclamation of the gospel. The church that is the ELCA threatening to tear itself apart over the issue of blessing same-sex unions, an issue that is not the gospel which constitutes and unites the church. That is the church which Jesus' resurrection frees you to love.

You are free to imprint on your hearts and minds the great apostolic words from Ephesians 4: "I therefore, the prisoner in the Lord, beg you to lead a life worthy of the calling to which you have been called, with all humility and gentleness, with patience, putting up with one another in love, making every effort to maintain the unity of the Spirit in the bond of peace." In the last chapter of Luke's Gospel, Jesus tells the disciple community to await being "clothed with power from on high." We do not need to be "clothed with power from on high" to join a bridge club, root for the Buckeyes, golf with our friends, or champion causes with other like-minded people.

But we need "power from on high" to be the church, that is, to be so grasped by Christ that we can "put up with each other" in "a community that can sustain its unity in the midst of disagreement over emotionally charged issues, without demonizing or disregarding, excluding or humiliating each other" (*Faithful Conversation*, Daniel Olson, page 102). Olson points out that our present situation gives the church a magnificent opportunity to be the church—to disagree profoundly over truly important matters without turning away from each other or turning against each other.

The resurrection of Jesus frees us to love the world.

I think of that great cosmic and mysterious universe set in motion by the creative urge of the Father, called into being through the creating Logos, given a life which is pointed toward a new heaven and a new earth by the aspiring Holy Spirit. But we are free to love a more manageable world, our own small planet placed into our care as stewards of God's gift. Such love of our world was never more in need.

I have noticed two insistent temptations in my illness. The first is an almost narcissistic fixation on myself and my body, noting every twinge and change, keeping my plumbing working, measuring what and how much I can eat.

The second is an irrational twist on "Stop the world, I want to get off." My cry, when I hear of plans for travel I will no longer be able to undertake, futures of which I will not be a part, is to shout, "Stop the world because I'm getting off."

What rescues me from both of these temptations is, in part, my longtime habit of watching the daily news, reading the daily paper, working my way through two news magazines, and keeping up with the affairs of the church and the world.

A lot of what I read is appalling in terms of our care for this planet. *Time* magazine had a cover story on Ann Coulter a few weeks ago. In the article she was quoted as saying: "God gave us the earth. We have dominion over the plants, the animals, the seas. God said, 'Earth is yours. Take it. Rape it. It's yours.'" To which Peter Fenn, her Democratic counterpart on a Fox news broadcast responded: "We're Americans, so we should consume as much of the earth's resources as fast as we possibly can." To which Coulter replied, "Yes. Yes! As opposed to living like the Indians" (*Time*, March 25, 2005, page 37). Coulter gets $25,000 a speech for throwing this "red meat" to her right-wing audiences. No politician would dare to say such things, but the audiences love it. What we must do is look at the policies proposed and imposed by law and decree, the lack of concern for pollution and our consumption of fossil fuels. The World-watch Institute publishes an annual "State of the World" report. The goal of the World-watch Institute is for our generation to hand on to future generations a world undiminished in its capacity to sustain life.

We are not on the verge of Armageddon. We are not waiting for Christ to rapture us out of the world so that we can have a ring-side seat as the world is destroyed. We are called to be stewards, to hand on a world as we received it from our parents and grandparents.

We are called to love the world, to want clean air and water for everyone, to give ourselves into the service of peace instead of blindly following our leaders in senseless wars, to commit to the cause of justice especially where our institutions and our country are guilty of injustice. That is a big order. But you are set free to pursue it by the resurrection of Christ, who has put an end to the dominion of death. We are free for the battle because the victory is already won.

So we come back to the beginning. My capacity for being a steward is limited and moving towards its end. Your capacity is still vibrant and active. But God continues to call all of us, even me counting my days, to be grasped by the great good news that Jesus is risen, to be taken up into Christ's offering in the meal, to be the church by putting up with each other in love, and to care for our world.

I am being readied for my final baptism, my last dying and rising with Christ. All my baptisms of dying and rising with Christ, from July 28, 1929, to the present moment, have prepared me for this time. I turn often to the hymn-prayer with which J.S. Bach concludes his magnificent Passion According to St. John. It is the final stanza of a hymn by Martin Schalling (1532-1608), hymn 325 in the *Lutheran Book of Worship*. I ask you to join me in praying/singing that final stanza.

> Lord, let at last thine angels come,
> To Abr'hams bosom bear me home,
> That I may die unfearing;
> And in its narrow chamber keep
> My body safe in quiet sleep
> Until thy reappearing.

And then from death awaken me,
That these mine eyes with joy may see,
O Son of God, thy glorious face,
My Savior and my fount of grace.
Lord Jesus Christ,
My prayer attend, my prayer attend,
And I will praise thee without end.

In the Name of the Father, and of the Son, and of the Holy Spirit.

Walter R. Bouman
Edward C. Fendt Emeritus Professor of Systematic Theology
Trinity Lutheran Seminary, Columbus, Ohio

Bibliography

Althaus, Paul. *The Theology of Martin Luther*. Philadelphia: Fortress Press, 1956.

Barth, Karl. "Faith as Knowledge." In *Dogmatics in Outline*. New York: Harper & Row, 1959.

Bouman, Walter R. "HTS 1041 Lecture Notes." In *HTS 1041*. Columbus, Ohio: Trinity Lutheran Seminary, Jan. 3 - March 6, 1996.

_____. "HTS 3041 Constructive Theology Lecture Notes." Columbus, Ohio: Trinity Lutheran Seminary, 1992.

Braaten, Carl E. *Principles of Lutheran Theology*. 2nd ed. Minneapolis: Fortress Press, 2007.

Childs, James M., Jr. *Ethics in the Community of Promise: Faith, Formation, and Decision*. 2nd ed. Minneapolis: Fortress Press, 2006.

_____. *The Way of Peace: Christian Life in the Face of Discord*. Minneapolis: Fortress Press, 2008.

Evangelical Lutheran Worship. Minneapolis: Augsburg Fortress, 2006.

Forde, Gerhard O. "Seventh Locus: The Work of Christ." In *Christian Dogmatics*, edited by Robert W. Jenson and Carl E. Braaten. Minneapolis: Fortress Press, 1984.

Grenz, Stanley J. *Rediscovering the Triune God: The Trinity in Contemporary Theology*. Minneapolis: Fortress Press, 2004.

Hall, Douglas John. "Part I: Creaturely Being." In *Professing the Faith: Christian Theology in a North American Context*. Minneapolis: Fortress Press, 1993.

Hample, Stuart, and Eric Marshall. *Children's Letters to God*. New York: Workman Publishing Company, 1991.

Haut, Ann M., ed. *Jesus Is Risen: Theology for the Church the Lifework and Teaching of the Rev. Dr. Walter R. Bouman, Thd.*, 2 vols. Minneapolis: Lutheran University Press, 2015.

Jenson, Robert W. *A Large Catechism*. Delhi, New York: American Lutheran Publicity Bureau, 1991.

Lathrop, Gordon W. *Holy Ground: A Liturgical Cosmology*. Minneapolis: Fortress, 2003.

Leaver, Robin. *Luther's Liturgical Music: Principles and Implications*. Grand Rapids: William B. Eerdmans Publishing Co., 2007.

Lewis, Bill. "Trinitarian Formula as Name of God." ELCA Conference of Bishops, 9/14/88.

Lewis, C.S. *The Screwtape Letters, with Screwtape Proposes a Toast*. San Francisco: Harper.

Lohse, Bernard. *Martin Luther's Theology: Its Historical and Systematic Development*. Minneapolis: Fortress Press, 1999.

Luther, Martin. "An Order of Mass and Communion for the Church at Wittenberg." In *Luther's Works 3*. Philadelphia: Fortress, 1965.

Lutheran Book of Worship. Minneapolis: Augsburg Publishing House, 1978.

Madsen, Anna. "Moral and Mortal Support: The Role of a Faith Community in Shaping Ethical Decisions." In *Stand Boldly: Lutheran Theology Faces the Postmodern World*, edited by Eric Trozzo. Berkeley, California: Three Trees Press, 2009.

Marty, Martin E. *Come and Grow with Us: New Member Basics*. Minneapolis: Augsburg Fortress, 1996.

Mendes-Flohr, Paul. "The Promises and Limitations of Interfaith Dialogue." In *Criterion*. Chicago: University of Chicago Divinity School, 2013.

Meuser, Fred W. *Luther the Preacher*. Minneapolis: Augsburg Publishing House, 1983.

Moe-Lobeda, Cynthia. *Healing a Broken World: Globalization and God*. Minneapolis: Fortress Press, 2002.

Moltmann, Jürgen. *The Coming of God: Christian Eschatology*. Translated by Margaret Kohl. Minneapolis: Fortress Press, 1996.

_____. *The Spirit of Life: A Universal Affirmation* Minneapolis: Fortress Press, 1992.

_____. *The Trinity and the Kingdom: The Doctrine of God*. Translated by Margaret Kohl. San Francisco: Harper & Row, 1981.

_____. *The Way of Jesus Christ*. Minneapolis: Fortress Press, 1990.

Moore, Archimandrite L. *St. Seraphim of Sarov: A Spiritual Biography*. Blanco, Texas: New Sarov Press, 1994.

Pannenberg, Wolfhart. *Jesus—God and Man*. Translated by Lewis L. Wilkins and Duane A. Priebe. Philadelphia: Westminster Press, 1968.

_____. *What Is Man? Contemporary Anthropology in Theological Perspective*. Translated by Duane A. Priebe. Philadelphia: Fortress Press, 1970.

Peters, Ted. *God as Trinity*. Louisville: Westminster/John Knox Press, 1993.

_____. *God the World's Future: Systematic Theology for a New Era*. 2nd ed. Minneapolis: Fortress Press, 2000.

Pless, John T. *Handling the Word of Truth: Law and Gospel in the Church Today*. St. Louis: Concordia Publishing House, 2004.

Powell, Mark Allan. *Chasing the Eastern Star: Adventures in Reader Response Criticism*. Louisville: Westminster John Knox, 2001.

_____. "Law and Gospel and the Interpretation of Scripture." In *Lutheran Perspectives on Biblical Interpretation*. Minneapolis: Lutheran University Press, 2010.

Putnam, Robert D. *American Grace: How Religion Divides and Unites Us*. New York: Simon & Schuster, 2010.

Raabe, Nancy M. *Carl Flentge Schalk: A Life in Song*. St. Louis: Concordia Publishing House, 2013.

Radtke, David C., ed. *Hearing the Word: Lutheran Hermeneutics: A Vision of Life Under the Gospel*. Minneapolis: Lutheran University Press, 2006.

Rahner, Karl. *The Trinity*. Translated by Joseph Donceel. New York: Crossroad, 2005.

Reed, Luther D. *The Lutheran Liturgy*. rev. ed. Philadelphia: Fortress Press, 1947.

"Rite for Holy Baptism." In *Evangelical Lutheran Worship*. Minneapolis: Augsburg Fortress.

Schalk, Carl. *Luther on Music: Paradigms of Praise*. St. Louis: Concordia Publishing House, 1988.

Schwarz, Jeffrey, and Sharon Begley. *The Mind and the Brain: Neuroplasticity and the Power of Mental Force* New York: Regan Books/HarperCollins, 2002.

"The Holy Spirit." In *Jesus Is Risen: Theology for the Church*, edited by Ann M. Haut. Minneapolis: Lutheran University Press, 2015.

Thurian, Max. *The Eucharistic Memorial: Part 2*. Translated by J. G. Davies. Richmond: John Knox, 1961.

Tickle, Phyllis. *The Great Emergence: How Christianity Is Changing and Why*. Peabody, Massachusetts: Baker Books, 2008.

Torvend, Samuel. *Luther and the Hungry Poor*. Minneapolis: Fortress Press, 2008.

Vajda, Jaroslav. *Sing Peace, Sing Gift of Peace: The Comprehensive Hymnary of Jaroslav J. Vajda*. St. Louis: Concordia Publishing House, 2003.

Walther, C.F.W. *The Proper Distinction Between Law and Gospel*. St. Louis: Concordia, 2004; lectures given in 1864-1865.

Wink, Walter. *Engaging the Powers: Discernment and Resistance in a World of Domination*. Minneapolis: Augsburg Fortress, 1992.

Worship Supplement. St. Louis: Concordia Publishing House, 1969.

Wright, Robert. *The Moral Animal: Evolutionary Psychology and Everyday Life*. New York: Vintage Books, 1995.

Contributors

Stephen Bouman is executive director of the Congregational and Synodical Mission unit of the ELCA, in which he directs all the domestic ministry of the church body. He served over twenty years in parish ministry in New York City and New Jersey, and as bishop of the Metropolitan New York Synod of the ELCA from 1996-2008. He has written books on parish ministry, the response of the church to the September 11, 2001, attacks in New York, and on immigration issues. His current book, *The Mission Table*, is being used in congregations and synods throughout the ELCA. He is the founder of the Diakonia lay training program. Stephen and his family currently live in Chicago.

John Buchanan is editor and publisher of *The Christian Century* and pastor emeritus at the Fourth Church of Chicago. He served as moderator for the 208th General Assembly of the Presbyterian Church (PCUSA) and as pastor of Broad Street Presbyterian Church, Columbus Ohio, 1974-1985, during which he became a close friend of Walter's.

James M. Childs, Jr., was the Edward C. Fendt Professor of Systematic Theology at Trinity Lutheran Seminary in Columbus, Ohio, from 2004 to 2011 and the Joseph A. Sittler Professor of Theology and Ethics at Trinity Seminary from 1998 to 2004. He received his BA from Concordia Senior College in 1961, his MDiv from Concordia Seminary, St. Louis, in 1965; his STM in 1966 from Union Theological Seminary, New York; and his PhD from the Lutheran School of Theology at Chicago in 1974. From 1978 to 1997 he served Trinity Seminary as Associate Professor and then Professor of Ethics. He also was director for Studies on Sexuality, Evangelical Lutheran Church in America from 2002-2005.

Gordon W. Lathrop is a retired ELCA pastor and professor of liturgy. Since his retirement in 2004 as professor emeritus at the Lutheran Theological Seminary at Philadelphia, he has also taught at Yale Divinity School, the St. Thomas Pontifical University in Rome, and the Virginia Theological Seminary. He is the author, among other books, of *Holy Things: A Liturgical Theology* (Fortress Press, 1993), *The Pastor: A Spirituality* (Fortress Press, 2006) and *the Four Gospels on Sunday: The New Testament and the Reform of Christian Worship* (Fortress Press, 2012). He lives in Arlington, Virginia.

Jonathan Linman is assistant to the bishop for faith and leadership formation in the Metropolitan New York Synod of the ELCA. Formerly he served as director of the Center for Christian Spirituality and professor of Ascetical Theology at The General Theological Seminary of the Episcopal Church, where Walter Bouman was frequently a visiting professor after his retirement. Jonathan is author of *Holy Conversation: Spirituality for Worship* (Fortress Press, 2010), and contributed commentaries on lectionary texts for Holy Week and Easter in Fortress Press' *New Proclamation: Year C 2013*. He is a graduate of Carleton College (BA), Trinity Lutheran Seminary (MDiv), and Duquesne University (MA and PhD). Jonathan also served in his first call as pastor of Bethlehem Lutheran Church in the inner city of Pittsburgh, Pennsylvania.

Anna Madsen is a "freelance theologian" living in Sioux Falls, South Dakota. After graduating from Trinity Lutheran Seminary in Columbus, Ohio, she served a small South Dakota parish before earning a PhD in systematic theology in Regensburg, Germany. Immediately prior to her return to teach at Augustana College, an accident killed her husband and severely injured her young son Karl. Daughter Else was eight months old at the time. This event shaped her theology and her life, not least of all by being the catalyst to create OMG: Center for Theological Conversation, a place for individuals and groups, laity and clergy, to come for questions, conversation, and study.

Mark Allan Powell is professor of New Testament at Trinity Lutheran Seminary and an internationally known biblical scholar. He is editor of the *HarperCollins Bible Dictionary* and author of more than twenty-five books on the Bible and religion, including the widely used textbook, *Introducing the New Testament* (Baker Academic). He has also written in the areas of spiritual formation (*Loving Jesus*), stewardship (*Giving To God*), and homiletics (*What Do They Hear? Bridging the Gap between Pulpit and Pew*). Powell's DVDs, *How Lutherans Understand the Bible,* have received widespread use throughout the ELCA and were excerpted for inclusion in the *Lutheran Study Bible* (Augsburg Fortress).

Michael Rinehart is bishop of the Texas-Louisiana Gulf Coast Synod, ELCA, which includes Houston and New Orleans. He received a bachelor of music in organ performance from Valparaiso University,. He received his master of divinity from Trinity Lutheran Seminary in Columbus, Ohio. He lives in Montgomery, Texas, with his wife and children.

A life-long Episcopalian and former white-collar crime prosecutor, there was probably nobody more surprised to find herself at Trinity Lutheran Seminary in the fall of 1995 than **Rebecca Robbins-Penneman**. At the time, she had no thought of being ordained, but she did have a lot of questions about the Christian faith and the church. In Walt, Becky found a blazing intellect and a beloved mentor. Becky's call to the priesthood eventually became clear, and Walt preached at Becky's ordination in 2001. Since seminary, Becky has served as a parish priest in Ohio and then in Florida, where she is now the rector of the Church of the Good Shepherd in Dunedin, near Tampa.

J. Robert Wright has higher degrees from Emory University, The General Theological Seminary, Oxford University, the Episcopal Seminary of the Southwest, Trinity Lutheran Seminary, and the Theological University of Bern (Switzerland). His tenure at The General Theological Seminary began in 1968. Since 2000 he has served as the official historiographer of the Episcopal Church. Recent books include *Readings for the Daily Office from the Early Church, An Ecumenical Guidebook to the Holy Sepulchre/The Church of the Resurrection in Jerusalem,* and *A Companion to Bede.* He has also compiled a large volume of translations of patristic commentaries on the wisdom literature.

Editors

Nancy M. Raabe, MTS, STM, Trinity Lutheran Seminary, is author of a critical biography of Carl Schalk and several volumes of devotions for church musicians. A rostered leader in the Evangelical Lutheran Church in America, she is Publications Advisor for the Association of Lutheran Church Musicians, edits ALCM's practical resource In Tempo, and frequently writes on the history and music of the church for the journal CrossAccent. A former classical music critic, her work has been published in the *Boston Globe,* the *Milwaukee Sentinel,* the *New York Times,* and *Opera News.*

Ann M. Haut, PhD, was Dr. Bouman's student at Trinity Lutheran Seminary in 1991-1992. Dr. Bouman served as the academic chair on her doctoral committee, and later asked her to compile his sytematic theology into books for entry-level seminary students and adult lay readers. The two volumes, *Jesus Is Risen: Theology for the Church*, were published in 2015 and are available through Lutheran University Press.

Endnotes

Mass of the Resurrection: Walter Richard Bouman
Stephen Bouman

1   *Seven Stanzas at Easter*, by John Updike

2   BWV 180.

Preface and Acknowledgments

3   Ann M. Haut, ed., *Jesus Is Risen: Theology for the Church: The Lifework and Teaching of the Rev. Dr. Walter R. Bouman, ThD* (Minneapolis: Lutheran University Press, 2015), vol. 1, 59.

Law and Gospel in Matthew: Implications for Hermeneutics
Mark Allan Powell

4   This article is based on a paper given to the Lutheran World Federation Third Conference on Hermeneutics held in Chicago in September, 2014. It is also being published in Craig Koester and Kenneth Mtata, eds., *To All Nations: Lutheran Hermeneutics and the Gospel of Matthew*. LWF Studies 01/2015.

5   See especially Dale C. Allison, *The New Moses: A Matthean Typology* (Minneapolis: Fortress Press, 1993); Benjamin Bacon, *Studies in Matthew* (London: Constable, 1930); Günther Bornkamm, Gerhard Barth, and Heinz Joachim Held, *Tradition and Interpretation in Matthew*, NTL (Philadelphia: Westminster, 1963); Blaine Charette, *The Theme of Recompense in Matthew's Gospel*, JSNTSup 79 (Sheffield: Sheffield Academic Press, 1992); O. Lamar Cope, *Matthew: A Scribe Trained for the Kingdom of Heaven*, CBQMS 5 (Washington, D.C.: Catholic Biblical Association, 1976); W. D. Davies, *The Setting of the Sermon on the Mount* (Cambridge: Cambridge University Press, 1964); Terence Donaldson, *Jesus on the Mountain: A Study in Matthean Theology*, JSNTSup 8 (Sheffield: JSOT Press, 1985); John P. Meier, *The Vision of Matthew: Christ, Church, and Morality in the First Gospel* (New York: Paulist, 1979); M. Palachuvattil, *"The One Who Does the Will of My Father": Distinguishing Character of Disciples according to Matthew: An Exegetical Theological Study*, TGST 154 (Rome: Editrice Pontifica Università Gregoriana, 2007).

6   Mark Allan Powell, "Law and Gospel and the Interpretation of Scripture," in *Lutheran Perspectives on Biblical Interpretation* (Minneapolis: Lutheran University Press, 2010), 36-58.

7   Carl E. Braaten, *Principles of Lutheran Theology*, 2nd ed. (Minneapolis: Fortress Press, 2007), 39. Luther himself said, "The true and proper function of the law is to accuse and to kill; but the function of the gospel is to make alive." WA 39, I, 363.

8   Paul Althaus, *The Theology of Martin Luther* (Philadelphia: Fortress Press, 1956), 256.

9   Walther offers a somewhat more detailed listing of the effects of law and gospel. The law demands but does not enable compliance; it hurls people into despair, for it diagnoses the disease without providing any cure; and it terrifies the conscience by producing contrition and offering no comfort. The gospel creates faith, stills every voice of accusation, and transforms people by planting love in their hearts and enabling them to do good works. See C.F.W. Walther, *The Proper Distinction between Law and Gospel* (St. Louis: Concordia, 2004; lectures given in 1864-1865), 16. Cf. John T. Pless, *Handling the Word of Truth: Law and Gospel in the Church Today* (St. Louis: Concordia Publishing House, 2004), 14-15.

10 So, Althaus: "Luther's distinction is clearly related to the content of proclamation" (269).

11 Such an equation is nevertheless common. In an instruction book for those new to Lutheranism, Martin Marty says, "Law represents the demands of God, and the gospel is the promises of God." See Martin E. Marty, *Come and Grow with Us: New Member Basics* (Minneapolis: Augsburg Fortress, 1996), 10. Of course, Marty is trying to state a complex matter in simple terms, but such a construal ultimately misses the point and creates hermeneutical problems, as we shall see.

12 Althaus says, "in terms of its content, the law is the eternal will of God" (252). The divine will, furthermore, is consummate with God's holy nature, such that what the law requires is not mere obedience to this or that regulation, but absolute holy perfection, equal to that of God. Nothing else can stand in God's sight. Nothing else satisfies. Nothing else is acceptable. Nothing else even qualifies for consideration.

13 Luther writes in his 1535 Galatians commentary, "Thus the first understanding and use of the Law is to restrain the wicked. For the devil reigns in the whole world and drives men to all sorts of shameful deeds. That is why God has ordained magistrates, parents, teachers, laws, shackles, and all civic ordinances, so that, if they cannot do any more, they will at least bind the hands of the devil and keep him from raging at will." (*LW* 26:309). See also, from the second Antinomian Disputation: "Political righteousness is good and worthy of praise, though it cannot stand in the sight of God." And: "Among men, temporal righteousness has its own honor and its own reward in this life, but not with God." WA 39, I, 441 and 456–57. Cf. Bernard Lohse, *Martin Luther's Theology: Its Historical and Systematic Development* (Minneapolis: Fortress Press, 1999), 271.

14 Again from the Galatians commentary: "The other use of the Law is the theological or spiritual one, which serves to increase transgressions. This is the primary purpose of the Law of Moses, that through it sin might grow and be multiplied, especially in the conscience . . . And so when the Law accuses and terrifies the conscience— "You must do this or that! You have not done so! Then

you are condemned to the wrath of God and to eternal death!"—then the Law is being employed in its proper use and for its proper purpose. Then the heart is crushed to the point of despair. This use and function of the Law is felt by terrified and desperate consciences . . . Therefore the Law is a hammer that crushes rocks, a fire, a wind, and a great and mighty earthquake that overturns mountains." (*LW* 26:309–310).

15 See Powell, "Law and Gospel and the Interpretation of Scripture, 38–43. In essence, the controversy owes to the fact that the word *law* is used with two different meanings. In the Formula of Concord, the word *law* means "biblical commandments". If those documents had simply used the word *commandments* rather than *law*, there never would have been a controversy. No one doubts that biblical commandments have an ethical and catechetical function. For example, in his section on the Ten Commandments in the *Small Catechism*, Luther repeatedly asks, "What does this mean?" and each time he says that the meaning of the commandment is that God wants us to *do* or *not do* something; he never says that the meaning of the commandment is that we should despair of works righteousness and realize our need for the gospel. But when the word *law* is taken to mean "anything that reveals God's otherness" = "anything that causes us to recognize our separation from God" = "anything that accuses us and condemns us"—when the word *law* has *that* meaning, as it does when Luther speaks of the word of God being law and gospel—then there can be no meaningful "third use" (hence the controversy). When we gaze in awe upon God's holiness, we do not take notes regarding this or that aspect of God's divine nature that we might, with a bit more effort, be able to emulate. No, we tremble at the horrifying realization that are not simply ignorant or ineffective or lackadaisical or unmotivated: we are, in fact, *sinners*, and nothing that lies within our power (not even perfect obedience to all the commandments, if such were within our power) can change this.

Among writers I have surveyed, only Lohse recognizes the terminological confusion that lies at the heart of the "third use of the law" debate. Almost as an aside, he indicates that when the "educative function" is in view, "it is better to speak of a commandment than of a law" (275). The function of a commandment *per se* is "announcement of the divine will" though in the process of serving this function, biblical commandments might simultaneously operate as *law*, i.e., in an "accusing" manner. So, I would add, might biblical promises, which also function primarily as announcements of the divine will.

16 In short, I believe there is a difference between *the law* and "laws." The distinction between the two is analogous to the difference between *sin* and "sins." Laws try to deal with the problem of sins. As Lutherans we are often quick to say that "laws" (or commandments) do not deal very effectively with sins because we are unable to keep these commandments or to obey these laws. That may often be true, but it is a limited, reductionist understanding of the problem. Even if we *were* able to keep all of the commandments—all of the "laws"—we would still be *sinners*. And this is what *the law* reveals—this is what *the law* that we refer to in "law and gospel" does—it reveals that we are sinners, quite apart from the fact that we fail to obey individual laws and often commit particular sins. We are not sinners because we sin; rather, we sin because we *are* sinners. And the *law* does not accuse us because it consists of laws; rather, "laws" accuse us because they

witness to *the law* (they bear witness to the holy righteousness of God in light of which all human merit is to be judged).

17 Some of the terminological confusion may result from the fact that Luther himself used the term *law* differently in some (earlier) writings than in other (later) ones. Hendrix suggests that Luther made up his hermeneutic of law and gospel as he went along, though from the outset he seems to have had a hermeneutical vision, particularly with regard to what life under the gospel should be. See Scott Hendrix, "The Interpretation of the Bible According to Luther and the Confessions, or Did Luther Have a (Lutheran) Hermeneutic?" in David C. Radtke, ed., *Hearing the Word: Lutheran Hermeneutics: A Vision of Life under the Gospel* (Minneapolis: Lutheran University Press, 2006), 13-31. In any case, subsequent reformers definitely used the term *law* differently than Luther did in his more mature writings on law and gospel.

18 Joachim Jeremias, *The Sermon on the Mount*. Facet Books (Philadelphia: Fortress Press, 1963).

19 Of course, the Formula of Concord would allow for two additional functions as well. The Sermon on the Mount and other Matthean texts do establish standards that might keep society from falling into total chaos, and believers who have been justified by grace will be interested in knowing the will of God so that they might strive (albeit unsuccessfully) to live as God would want. But these are extra, "bonus" functions; according to Lutheran scholasticism, the most important function of the Sermon on the Mount was always to reveal the holy will of God in a way that exposes sin and brings sinners to despair of anything save trust in Christ alone.

20 Jeremias was a Lutheran himself, so the error is not inevitable. Indeed, Martin Luther's own reflections on the Sermon on the Mount are completely free of this "Lutheran error."

21 Althaus says that, for Luther, Jesus' Sermon on the Mount sharpened the demands of the law to the point that "sinful man . . . simply cannot fulfill it" (254; cf. *WA* 39, I, 364, 374). Still, it is likely that both Jesus and the Matthean evangelist assumed their audiences would be able to keep these demands in the only manner that would have made sense within a context of Torah-observant Judaism: they would orient their lives in accord with a commitment to observe the prescriptions and proscriptions of their rabbi's teaching on a day-to-day basis, asking forgiveness for specific instances of failure when those occurred.

22 Without being quite so cavalier, Forde dismisses Jesus' claim that all biblical commandments will remain until heaven and earth pass away (Matthew 5:17-18) by insisting that "'heaven and earth' *do* 'pass away' in the eschatological fulfillment anticipated and grasped by faith" (447). This strikes me as a desperate attempt to reconcile Matthew with Paul (specifically Romans 10:4), though Forde's concern was probably more theological than exegetical: he wanted to reconcile the Matthean attitude toward commandments with the Lutheran concept of "law and gospel." In either case, there is special pleading. A more helpful approach would be to recognize that Matthew probably means something different by "commandments" than either Paul or Luther meant by "law." But the root problem lies in trying to use the homiletical principle

of "law and gospel" (concerned with the reception of texts) as an exegetical principle (for determining the intended meaning of texts).

23 As I have explained elsewhere, if we truly embraced the hermeneutic of authorial intent that we often espouse, we would have to reject all christological interpretations of the Old Testament (including those proffered by New Testament authors). See Mark Allan Powell, *Chasing the Eastern Star: Adventures in Reader Response Criticism* (Louisville: Westminster John Knox, 2001), 176-79.

24 In Lutheran tradition, the goal of a sermon is not to provide people with doctrinal or moral instruction: *preaching* is different from *teaching*. This, of course, does not mean that sermons have no element of instruction. According to Meuser, Luther typically viewed the sermon as "comprised of teaching and exhortation." But, in practice, Meuser continues, "that's not the way Luther preached. He preached as if the sermon were not a classroom, but instead a battleground! Every sermon was a battle for the souls of the people." See Fred W. Meuser, *Luther the Preacher* (Minneapolis: Augsburg Publishing House, 1983), 25.

25 The preacher will sometimes justify this by saying, "I am preaching the third use of the law," which is at least part of "law and gospel." I disagree. Didactic sermons focus on the third use of "commandments" (which is actually the primary function of commandments) but which has nothing to do with "law and gospel."

26 Reader-response criticism is often associated with either a) a postmodern hermeneutic that denies the stability and/or accessibility of meaning, and/or b) ideological approaches to texts (feminist, Marxist, etc.) that seek to impose lenses for understanding in ways that overtly reject or resist authorial intent. But, though reader-response criticism may be popular with scholars who operate with a postmodern or ideological hermeneutic, the approach itself assumes no particular epistemology. As a mode of literary analysis, reader response criticism simply employs various strategies for discerning anticipated effects of texts on various readers and identifying factors that make certain effects likely to be realized. See Powell, *Chasing the Eastern Star*.

27 In my own teaching, I summarize the text-to-sermon process thus: First, scripture should be faithfully exegeted in accord with the historical-critical method, so as to reveal the basic intentions of its original author. Then, we may employ reader response criticism to take a second step: drawing upon insights from pastoral theology, and using gifts of discernment acquired through years of exercising empathetic, prayerful concern for other people, we should be able to discern a plurality of possible effects that the text might have on people in various contexts. From that plurality of possible effects, we should isolate "potential effects that would be congruent with authorial intent," even if they go beyond the specifics of such intent. Finally, from the limited plurality of "potential effects congruent with authorial intent," the Lutheran preacher will focus on those effects that are always the intended impact of any Lutheran sermon: the accusatory effects of law and the comforting effects of gospel.

28 So Althaus: "For Luther, then, God's word can, in the final analysis, definitely not be categorized into law and gospel. The one and the same word strikes

sinful man both as law and as gospel" (264). The functions of law and gospel "are functions of the same word. They always take place concurrently" (265). Also Lohse: "The distinction between law and gospel cannot be made once for all, but must be drawn ever anew . . . What is further unique about Luther's distinction is that law and gospel cannot be assigned to the Old or New Testament, nor to particular biblical passages, so as to establish for all time that one text is only law and the other gospel. Most texts assigned to the law have also a gospel side, and most texts assigned to the gospel have also a law side . . . Luther's distinction is clearly related to the context of proclamation" (269). Walther suggests that the choice of preaching law or gospel be determined by need of the audience: "the law is to be preached to secure sinners and the gospel to alarmed sinners" (17). But it seems to me that most congregations may contain both types of sinners and that individual sinners may experience both security and alarm within the course of a single sermon.

From Resurrection to Trinity
James M. Childs, Jr.

29 Ann M. Haut, ed., *Jesus Is Risen: Theology for the Church: The Lifework and Teaching of the Rev. Dr. Walter R. Bouman, ThD*, 2 vols. (Minneapolis: Lutheran University Press, 2015).

30 Wolfhart Pannenberg, *Jesus—God and Man*, trans. Lewis L. Wilkins and Duane A. Priebe (Philadelphia: Westminster Press, 1968), 67-69. The points in italics are quotes; comments are brief paraphrases of the essential points of Pannenberg's commentary.

31 The discussion of theological anthropology that follows draws on James M. Childs, Jr. *Christian Anthropology and Ethics* (Philadelphia: Fortress Press, 1978), especially 98-99 and 103-117.

32 Wolfhart Pannenberg, *What Is Man? Contemporary Anthropology in Theological Perspective*, trans. Duane A. Priebe (Philadelphia: Fortress Press, 1970), 28-40.

33 Stanley J. Grenz, *Rediscovering the Triune God: The Trinity in Contemporary Theology* (Minneapolis: Fortress Press, 2004), 6.

34 Ibid., 5. Karl Barth, "Faith as Knowledge," in *Dogmatics in Outline* (New York: Harper & Row, 1959). provides a helpful brief expression of the point Grenz is making in this quote.

35 Karl Rahner, *The Trinity*, trans. Joseph Donceel (New York: Crossroad, 2005), 18.

36 Ibid.

37 Ibid., xv.

38 Ibid., 21-22.

39 Ibid., 24.

40 Ted Peters, *God the World's Future: Systematic Theology for a New Era*, 2nd ed. (Minneapolis: Fortress Press, 2000), 113e.

41 Jürgen Moltmann, *The Trinity and the Kingdom: The Doctrine of God*, trans. Margaret Kohl (San Francisco: Harper & Row, 1981), 129.

42 Ibid., 174-175.

43 Ibid., 112.

44 Ibid., 25ff.

45 Quoted in Peters, op.cit., 207.

46 Moltmann, *The Trinity and the Kingdom*, 23.

47 Jürgen Moltmann, *The Coming of God: Christian Eschatology*, trans. Margaret Kohl (Minneapolis: Fortress Press, 1996), 270-79.

48 James M. Childs, Jr., *The Way of Peace: Christian Life in the Face of Discord* (Minneapolis: Fortress Press, 2008), 74.

49 Moltmann, *The Trinity and the Kingdom*, 158.

50 James M. Childs, Jr., *Ethics in the Community of Promise: Faith, Formation, and Decision*, 2nd ed. (Minneapolis: Fortress Press, 2006), 51.

The Crisis of the Offertory: A Treasured Conversation with Walter R. Bouman

Gordon W. Lathrop

51 For example, in a book Walt had used in teaching, *Holy Things: A Liturgical Theology* (Minneapolis: Fortress, 1993), 139-158, and also in "The Bodies on Nevado Ampato: A Further Note on Offering and Offertory," *Worship* (71:6, 1997), 546-554.

52 Both the idea and Bouman's estimation of its importance are clearly expressed in his posthumous systematic theology, edited by Ann M. Haut, *Jesus is Risen: Theology for the Church* (Minneapolis: Lutheran University Press, 2015), vol. 2, 175-176.

53 "An Order of Mass and Communion for the Church at Wittenberg," in *Luther's Works 3* (Philadelphia: Fortress Press, 1965), 25-26.

54 On Luther, eucharist and the community chest, see especially Samuel Torvend, *Luther and the Hungry Poor* (Minneapolis: Fortress, 2008).

55 Max Thurian, *The Eucharistic Memorial: Part 2*, trans. J. G. Davies (Richmond: John Knox, 1961), 107.

56 Thurian, *loc. cit.*

57 Thurian, *The Eucharistic Memorial: Part 2*, 18.

58 Luther D. Reed, *The Lutheran Liturgy*, rev. ed. (Philadelphia: Fortress Press, 1947), 310-11.

59 *Worship Supplement* (St. Louis: Concordia Publishing House, 1969).

60 In the *LBW*, "Create in me . . ." (Psalm 51:10-12) was reserved to be used at a service where there was no communion. "The sacrifices of God . . ." (Psalm 51:17-19b) was dropped.

61 *Lutheran Book of Worship* (Minneapolis: Augsburg Publishing House, 1978), 67-68.

62 See Ann M. Haut, ed., *Jesus Is Risen: Theology for the Church: The Lifework and Teaching of the Rev. Dr. Walter R. Bouman, ThD*, 2 vols. (Minneapolis: Lutheran University Press, 2015).

63 Gordon W. Lathrop, *Holy Ground: A Liturgical Cosmology* (Minneapolis: Fortress Press, 2003), 148-52.

64 *Evangelical Lutheran Worship* (Minneapolis: Augsburg Fortress, 2006), 106.

65 Ibid., "Service Music," #181-188

The Holy Spirit and the Church as Eschatological Community
Jonathan Linman

66 "The Holy Spirit," in Ann M. Haut, ed., *Jesus Is Risen: Theology for the Church: The Lifework and Teaching of the Rev. Dr. Walter R. Bouman, ThD* (Minneapolis: Lutheran University Press, 2015), vol. 2.

67 Ibid., 12ff., where Walter explores the coming of the Holy Spirit as the inauguration of the messianic age.

68 Ibid., 1.

69 Ibid., 15, where Walter makes the point that for Paul, the Holy Spirit's dwelling happens to the disciples as a community, and that this dwelling of the Spirit is furthermore characterized by sociality, ibid., 16.

70 Ibid., 4, where Walter quotes Jürgen Moltmann, "God's eternity now took the place of God's future, heaven replaced the coming kingdom, the spirit that redeems the soul from the body supplanted the Spirit as 'the well of life,' the immortality of the soul displaced the resurrection of the body, and the yearning for another world become a substitute for changing this one." Jürgen Moltmann, *The Spirit of Life: A Universal Affirmation* (Minneapolis: Fortress Press, 1992).

71 Ibid., 2-5.

72 Ibid., 12, where Walt makes a similar point about the Spirit at creation.

73 Ibid.

74 Ibid. 10, where Walter quotes Robert Jenson who makes the point about the Spirit being centered in Jesus whom God the Father sent: "That is, he is God's spirit and therefore not one of the numerous spirits of this variously and ambiguously animated creation. . . . To be in this Spirit, the Spirit the creed has in mind, is to be disciples of the one whose Spirit he is, of the Lord Jesus and none other," Robert W. Jenson, *A Large Catechism* (Delhi, New York: American Lutheran Publicity Bureau, 1991).

75 Ibid., where Walter discusses at length this contemporary re-appropriation of the meaningfulness of the word 'spirit.'

76 Ibid., 13.

77 A nod to the hymn, "God, My Lord, My Strength" by Jiří Třanovsky (1636), stanza 3: "Up, weak knees and spirit bowed in sorrow! No tomorrow shall arise to beat you down; God goes before you and angels all around; on your head a crown!" hymn 795 God, My Lord, My Strength," in *Evangelical Lutheran Worship* (Minneapolis: Augsburg Fortress, 2006). Walter also makes the point (see note 60, following) that the Spirit as Advocate is the one "to hold you up when your legs are weak and crumbling."

78 Ibid., 2 and 22.

79 Ibid., 13.

80 Ibid.

81 Ibid., 1, and as quoted in the introduction to this essay.

82 Ibid., 13-14.

83 Ibid., 15.

84 Ibid., 16.

85 "Rite for Holy Baptism," in *Evangelical Lutheran Worship* (Minneapolis: Augsburg Fortress), 229.

86 Ibid., 14.

87 In the Smalcald Articles, Luther lists among the means of grace, confession and forgiveness, alongside preaching, baptism, Eucharist and mutual conversation and consolation among the brothers and sisters.

88 Rooted in Matthew 18:20, Luther in the Smalcald Articles also lists as a means of grace mutual conversation and consolation among the brothers and sisters, a practice known in Christian communities, namely, the church, the monastery, and the home.

89 Ibid., 12.

90 Ibid., 16, where Walter also discusses Luther's "double thesis": "A Christian is a perfectly free lord of all, subject to none. A Christian is a perfectly dutiful servant of all, subject to all," from Luther's treatise, "Freedom of a Christian," *Luther's Works*, Vol. 31, 344.

91 The Small Catechism was intended for instruction in the home. Luther arguably translated his communal experience as an Augustinian Friar to that of husband and father with domestic duties in the family at home.

92 Ibid., 17.

93 Ibid., 13.

94 This humorous quip from Walter's mouth came in the context of one of his lectures during the course, "Spirituality and the Eucharist," taught at The General Theological Seminary in New York City, a year or two before his death.

95 Archimandrite L. Moore, *St. Seraphim of Sarov: A Spiritual Biography* (Blanco, Texas: New Sarov Press, 1994), 126. Reportedly an alternate translation of the Russian is closer to the point that the Holy Spirit produces numerical growth: "Acquire the Holy Spirit and thousands around you will be saved."

96 Ibid., 17.

97 The church as genuine community and not a club of the like-minded was a central focus of the last sermon I heard Walter preach. This was the William Reed Huntington Memorial Sermon at Grace Episcopal Church in New York City, and took place so many months before Walter's death.

All Life is Sacramental
Michael Rinehart

98 *Tractates on the Gospel of John*, 80:3.

99 The Apology of the Augsburg Confession, XIII:6.

100 *The Babylonian Captivity of the Church*, LW 36:91.

101 Ibid.

102 Ibid.

103 Ibid., LW 36:94.

104 From dictionary.reference.com/browse/holy-sacraments.

105 The Apology of the Augsburg Confession, Article XIII.

106 *Evangelical Lutheran Worship*, Leaders Edition, Proper Preface for Christmas, 270.

107 Edited by Ann M. Haut, Lutheran University Press, 2015.

108 Ibid., Vol. 2, Chapter 7.

Walter Bouman: A Reflection
John Buchanan

109 Stuart Hample and Eric Marshall, *Children's Letters to God* (New York: Workman Publishing Company, 1991).

110 Phyllis Tickle, *The Great Emergence: How Christianity Is Changing and Why* (Peabody, Massachusetts: Baker Books, 2008).

111 Robert D. Putnam, *American Grace: How Religion Divides and Unites Us* (New York: Simon & Schuster, 2010).

112 Paul Mendes-Flohr, "The Promises and Limitations of Interfaith Dialogue," in *Criterion* (Chicago: University of Chicago Divinity School, 2013).

Trinity: Why "Abba"?
Becky Robbins-Penniman

113 See, for example, Mary Daly in Walter R. Bouman, "HTS 1041 Lecture Notes," in HTS 1041 (Trinity Lutheran Seminary, Columbus, OH, January 3 – March 6, 1996), Lecture 18, 5.

114 Bouman, HTS 3041 "Constructive Theology Lecture Notes," (Columbus, OH: Trinity Lutheran Seminary, 1992), Outline p. 5. See also Bouman, "HTS 1041 Lecture Notes," Lectures 17 and 18.

115 Ibid.

116 Bouman, "HTS 1041 Lecture Notes," Lecture 18, 5-7.

117 Ted Peters, *God as Trinity* (Louisville: Westminster/John Knox Press, 1993), 91.

118 See generally Douglas John Hall, "Part I: Creaturely Being," in *Professing the Faith: Christian Theology in a North American Context* (Minneapolis: Fortress Press, 1993).

119 See Lecture 6, p. 1, quoting John Wheeler in Bouman, "HTS 1041 Lecture Notes."

120 This concept comes from Raimundo Panikkar; see Peters, *God as Trinity*, 74-75.

121 This has been a classic description of what Jesus does with regard to God; see Ibid., 209, note 120.

122 Bouman, "HTS 1041 Lecture Notes," Lecture 17, p. 7 quoting Jenson.

123 Jürgen Moltmann, *The Way of Jesus Christ* (Minneapolis: Fortress Press, 1990), 289.

124 See Lecture 12, p. 2 in Bouman, "HTS 1041 Lecture Notes." See also, Gerhard O. Forde, "Seventh Locus: The Work of Christ," in *Christian Dogmatics*, ed. Robert W. Jenson and Carl E. Braaten (Minneapolis: Fortress Press, 1984), 92.

125 See Lecture 13, p. 6-7 in Bouman, "HTS 1041 Lecture Notes."

126 Forde, "Seventh Locus: The Work of Christ," 91.

127 See Lecture 12, p. 6 in Bouman, "HTS 1041 Lecture Notes."

128 See Lecture 18, p. 5 in Ibid.

129 See Lecture 12, p. 7 in Ibid.

130 C.S. Lewis, *The Screwtape Letters, with Screwtape Proposes a Toast* (San Francisco: Harper).

131 Peters, *God as Trinity*, 92.

132 See, generally, Walter Wink, *Engaging the Powers: Discernment and Resistance in a World of Domination* (Minneapolis: Augsburg Fortress, 1992).

133 Bill Lewis, "Trinitarian Formula as Name of God" (ELCA Conference of Bishops, 9/14/88).

134 Wink, *Engaging the Powers: Discernment and Resistance in a World of Domination*, 319-20.

135 Ibid., 305.

Misdirected Trust or Misfiring Neurons: Theology and Science and a Study of Sin
Anna Madsen

136 Jeffrey Schwarz and Sharon Begley, *The Mind and the Brain: Neuroplasticity and the Power of Mental Force* (New York: Regan Books/HarperCollins, 2002), 286.

137 Walter R. Bouman, Lecture Notes, HTS 1041, Trinity Lutheran Seminary, Columbus, Ohio.

138 Robert Wright, *The Moral Animal: Evolutionary Psychology and Everyday Life* (New York: Vintage Books, 1995), 9.

139 Ibid., 220-222.

140 Ibid., 223.

141 Ibid., 348.

142 Schwarz and Begley, *The Mind and the Brain: Neuroplasticity and the Power of Mental Force* 19.

143 Ibid., 32-33.

144 Ibid., 24-25.

145 Ibid., 36.

146 Ibid., 19.

147 Ibid., 55.

148 Ibid., 264.

149 Ibid., 283.

150 Anna Madsen, "Moral and Mortal Support: The Role of a Faith Community in Shaping Ethical Decisions," in *Stand Boldly: Lutheran Theology Faces the Postmodern World*, ed. Eric Trozzo (Berkeley, California: Three Trees Press, 2009), 205-218.

151 Schwartz and Begley, *The Mind and the Brain: Neuroplasticity and the Power of Mental Force*, 320.

152 Ibid., 321.

153 Cynthia Moe-Lobeda, *Healing a Broken World: Globalization and God* (Minneapolis: Fortress Pres, 2002).

Dying and Living
Nancy Raabe

154 Ann M. Haut, ed., *Jesus is Risen: Theology for the Church: The Lifework and Teaching of Rev. Dr. Walter R. Bouman, ThD* (Minneapolis: Lutheran University Press, 2015), vol. 1, 147.

155 Paul in Romans 6: "But if we have died with Christ, we believe that we will also live with him. We know that Christ, being raised from the dead, will never die again; death no longer has dominion over him. The death he died, he died to sin, once for all; but the life he lives, he lives to God. So you also must consider yourselves dead to sin and alive to God in Christ Jesus."

156 Conversation with the author, June 25, 2015.

157 Carl Schalk, "The Church's Song: Proclamation, Pedagogy and Praise," article for the forthcoming LSB companion (St. Louis: Concordia Publishing House).

158 "Basic Lutheran Understandings of Music in Worship," address at the biennial conference of the Association of Lutheran Church Musicians, San Diego, California, June 28, 2003.

159 Haut, *Jesus Is Risen*, vol. 1, 116.

160 Luther never intended to become a "composer," but wrote music for practical purposes only. To Luther's surprise, his first two hymns of many to come, written in the prolific year of 1523—"A New Song Here Has Now Begun" (the structure of which "A Mighty Fortress" was to echo years later) and "Dear Christians, One and All, Rejoice"—proved enormously popular, and the pub-

lic demanded more. Yet Luther always considered himself an amateur musician in the true sense of that word, one with a deep love for the subject. After hearing a group of Senfl's motets it was reported that Luther said, "I would not be able to compose such a motet, even if I would tear myself to pieces in the attempt" —adding shrewdly, "just as he [Senfl] would not be able to preach a Psalm as I can." Robin Leaver, *Luther's Liturgical Music: Principles and Implications* (Grand Rapids: William B. Eerdmans Publishing Co., 2007), 58-59.

161 For example, Bouman has said that "Martin Luther identified 'heaven' with the creedal and biblical phrase, 'the right hand of God,' which he takes from Psalm 98:1: 'O sing to the Lord a new song, for he has done marvelous things. His right hand and his holy arm have gotten him victory.' For Luther, the 'right hand' is where God is gaining the victory *through the saving event of Jesus as the Christ"*(emphasis added). Haut, *Jesus Is Risen*, vol. 1, 123-24.

162 Robin Leaver, *Luther's Liturgical Music: Principles and Implications* (Grand Rapids: William B. Eerdmans Publishing Co., 2007), 52.

163 See Bouman's quotation of this passage in this volume, page 197.

164 Luther's motet is titled *Non moriar sed vivam* and is reproduced in Leaver, ibid., 60.

165 Ibid.

166 Ibid.

167 Ibid.

168 Carl Schalk, *Luther on Music: Paradigms of Praise* (St. Louis: Concordia Publishing House, 1988), 9.

169 Reproduced in Leaver, op. cit., 53.

170 A deft performance of Luther's *Non moriar* at an appropriately brisk tempo can be heard on the penultimate track on the multi-disc set *Martin Luther: Hymns, Ballads, Chants, Truth*, released by Concordia Publishing House in 2004.

171 Actually the third line of stanza 1 originally read "A tardy worshipper." It is crossed out in Schalk's annotated copy of the text and replaced by "A pilgrim strangely stirred." Original letter housed in the Schalk archives at the Center for Church Music, Concordia University Chicago. See cuchicago.edu/about-concordia/center-for-church-music.

172 "Those big soaring lines!" Schalk once said. "I've always been partial to long lines. Because when you have those, you've got room to develop a good melody." See Nancy Raabe, *Carl Schalk: A Life in Song* (St. Louis: Concordia Publishing House, 2013), 104. ,

173 In music theory this gesture is called an *échappée,* or *escape tone,* when a note "escapes" from an otherwise stepwise melodic line.

174 The composer had long admired Schalk's instincts. Of the best-known hymn by Vajda and Schalk, "Now the Silence," Vajda later wrote that "Carl Schalk must be given credit for recognizing the potential of this hymn. Its subsequent acceptance convinced me (and evidently many others) that hymns could take

on new forms and yet perform their function in congregational worship." Jaroslav Vajda, *Sing Peace, Sing Gift of Peace: The Comprehensive Hymnary of Jaroslav J. Vajda* (St. Louis: Concordia Publishing House, 2003), 175.

175 Housed in the Carl Schalk archives at the Center for Church Music on the campus of Concordia University Chicago.

176 Documents relating to the genesis of this work may be found in the Carl Schalk manuscript archives, at the Center for Church Music on campus of Concordia University Chicago. See www.cuchicago.edu/centerforchurchmusic.

177 Interview with the author, December 4, 2012.

178 Housed in the Carl Schalk archives at the Center for Church Music.

179 Ibid. Emphasis is Vajda's.

180 Haut, *Jesus Is Risen*, vol. 1, 117.

Biography: Walter R. Bouman

181 Adapted and expanded from the ELCA News Service, August 19, 2005, found at www.elca.org/News-and-Events/5533.

182 The hymn festival in April 2001 at Trinity Lutheran Seminary in Columbus, Ohio, sponsored by the Association of Lutheran Church Musicians, featured Bouman reading his own narration. It was produced as a compact disc, "Joy Is Sounding," that may be ordered from ALCM by calling 1-800-624-2526 or by visiting http://www.alcm.org/marketplace/recordings/.

183 Paul F. M. Zahl, *Anglican Theological Review*, Vol. 82, No. 3 (Summer 2000). Bouman's book is published by the American Lutheran Publicity Bureau.